Beachcruising

An Illustrated Guide to the Boats, Gear,
Navigation Techniques, Cuisine, and
Comforts of Small Boat Cruising

Douglas Alvord

International Marine Publishing
Camden, Maine

Published by International Marine Publishing

10 9 8 7 6 5 4 3 2 1

Copyright © 1992 International Marine Publishing, an imprint of TAB
BOOKS. TAB BOOKS is a division of McGraw-Hill, Inc.

Library of Congress Cataloging-in-Publication Data
Alvord, Douglas,
    Beachcruising : an illustrated guide to the boats, gear,
navigation techniques, cuisine, and comforts of small boat cruising
/ Douglas Alvord.
        p.   cm.
    Includes index.
    ISBN 0-87742-973-1
    1. Boats and boating   2. Sailing.   I. Title.
GV775.A38   1992
797.1 — dc20   91-36395
                                                                          CIP

Questions regarding the content of this book should be addressed to:

International Marine Publishing
P.O. Box 220
Camden, ME 04843

To a good friend, who experienced being on the water with appreciation and great pleasure, and whose spirit will always be outward bound.

Contents

Acknowledgments

Books are always the product of many hands, and while I'll own that writing and illustrating this one was a great deal of pleasure for me, it was the experience of working with a good editorial and production staff that has given it form and substance. Jim Babb's personal style of editing meshed well with my own intent, and his editorial notes to me themselves make interesting reading. I enjoyed, too, the "editorial conferences" aboard *White Heron*. My thanks to Jon Eaton for his indulgence, as *Beachcruising* was undertaken in much the same laid-back spirit as its text, returning dockside a bit tardy—hopefully reflective of the philosophy I've tried to espouse.

My appreciation as well to the International Marine staff, including Tom McCarthy for his careful copyediting, and Janet Robbins, who oversaw production.

Edith Allard has done her usual fine book design, for which she is well noted.

Foreword

"Small is beautiful."

And so it is with boats. Forget the hassle of the cruising yacht and all its high-tech gear. Forget the annual boatyard bill that weighs on heart and purse.

Go light! From kayaks to pocket cruisers, under paddle, oar, and sail, there are happy people out there exploring the coasts. Because their boats take so little maintenance, they can spend more time afloat. Because their boats are so small, they are closer to what they came to see. There is no cove, no creek, no saltmarsh or trickle where they cannot safely cruise.

I remember my fiftieth birthday, off a small island in Casco Bay, rowing the coast of Maine in a 15-foot Matinicus peapod. My sleeping bag and pack were in the bow, ready to toss ashore. As I rested on the oars, glistening drops chased each other into ever-widening circles on the quiet waters. The boat lay comfortably in the gentle surge along white granite shores; dark green spruce on the hill, the pungent salt smell of seaweed, and the loon's cry—as close to perfection as a man can get.

And all of this is yours, if you stir yourself ever so little.

Listen to Doug Alvord, who knows.

Hank Taft
Camden, Maine
(author, *A Cruising Guide to the Maine Coast*)

Introduction

There is a sense of discovery and anticipation when sailing up to an island for the first time—watching the low, gray-green form on the horizon take shape as you slowly approach; smelling the dense firs and kelp beds and wild roses; seeing an osprey or a small flock of sandpipers take flight over what looks to be a good landing spot.

The mainsheet is let go and the centerboard raised as the boat drifts the last few yards to the gravel beach; a few good pulls on the bow line and you are ashore. It's time to have a look about to see if this is where you feel like spending the night. Perhaps there is a dense, intriguing forest to explore; maybe the flats just beyond the kelp ledges look like a good spot for clams or mussels. And if this island doesn't have just what you thought it might, there's another just to the north, a half-hour's sail at most. Beachcruising is about time out, not schedules and destinations.

If it isn't too large, walking the perimeter of a "new" island is a good way to investigate its charms and see what wildlife and flora it harbors.

The sun is beginning to recede into the western horizon, and the southwesterly breeze that brought you here has all but given way to stillness, leaving just the gentle lapping of small waves on the pebble beach. The kelp swishes back and forth in the low surf as the tide comes in, and as you watch the shorebirds skimming the water, you begin to set up camp for the night. Soon an elegant meal is on the portable stove—no beans and hot dogs tonight: there were fine mussels to be had for the taking; a decent bottle of wine is cooling in a tidal pool. There is time to think, perhaps to write out some thoughts; time to talk quietly about things for which the hectic life ashore leaves little time. Perhaps this is also a time for lovers.

Morning might break splendidly with a clear bright day and a fresh breeze or it might not; perhaps the trip home will be a little work and nature's schedule will become your own. At any rate you haven't gone far enough to make your return a hard chance. Snugged into some good foul-weather gear, even a little sailing in the rain is endurable if you retain your sense of humor.

There are many variations on the theme, but I think this is the essence of beachcruising: time and simplicity, small adventures with little fuss. All you need is a simple but able boat, some good, well-chosen gear, and a relatively unambitious itinerary. Beachcruising is not a goal-oriented activity; it is a quiet voyage of reflection.

When I was a teenager I did a little beachcruising in an old skiff with a jury-rigged sail, a heavy canvas army pup-tent, some canned goods, and nothing you could properly call foul-weather gear. Without the capacity of youth to have a good time no matter what, it could hardly be called "carefree cruising." The flat-bottom boat was leaky, cranky on *all* points of sail, and very wet to windward. Although my spirit of adventure might point my bow toward some ideal little cove alongshore, I seldom arrived there, despite tacking back and forth all afternoon with my destination in sight. Instead, I'd settle for wherever I could land, setting up camp with by then very soggy gear. If I couldn't manage a fire, I'd devour my food right from the can, then try to sleep in damp blankets and a leaky tent.

Of course I would not tell the story this way when I got home, although my grubby appearance usually gave me away—I hardly resembled the natty yachtsman back from a tidy sail. Still, I was on my own, and in its fashion it was fun, poorly equipped and badly planned though it may have been. Perhaps I'm still driven by the same spirit that made me want to go voyaging then, although given the wisdom of years I'd like to think this book contains some ideas that made *carefree cruising* a truer definition of the activity.

Boats is boats, they say, but some boats is more boat than others. On the one hand I'm prepared to say that if it floats you can probably have fun with it—for an afternoon anyway—and being out on the water is better than being home glued to the tube. But whether you cruise in a canoe, a rowing craft, a daysailer, or a runabout, it is wise to find a boat tailored to your actual needs. We'll look at some examples of each type later. Although specific models will be profiled, this is by no means a shopping guide. Rather, it is a description of what to look for—based on your own interests and abilities. In a like manner we will examine the gear and equipment that can turn a proper boat into a comfortable casual cruiser.

It would be wonderful if we worked only when the weather was lousy, leaving us free to play in the sunshine and scud along under fluffy cumulus clouds, with just the right amount of warm, sweet breeze to push us to that perfect beach. But real life doesn't work that way; despite the miracle of modern satellites, the fair weekend promised us by the smiling six-o'clock weatherman on Friday often turns gray and soggy by Sunday morning.

Not to worry. The history of boating has proved that most boats are more seaworthy than their skippers. With a little experience, contingency planning, and some decent seat-of-the-pants weather smarts you can shrug off the nasty stuff with a minimum of fuss. Weather and navigation are as important to the coastal, lake, or inland sailor as they are to the offshore mariner. Just because you are in sight of land doesn't mean you can always avoid difficult situations. Safety at sea is a cardinal concern; we will discuss how it applies to your scaled down adventuring in a commonsense fashion.

There are two other major areas I'd like to think are key to this type of cruising. The first is a matter of consequence: our environment. We are blessed with an almost infinite variety of waterways, islands, bays, and beaches along which to practice this freestyle recreation. While there are restrictions regarding access and private property, much of the area is open to us without charge, save our own restraint and conscience. But nothing on this Earth is really without charge. I'd like to suggest that our fee be the coin of respect. By learning about our cruising environment and how to take care of it, we become — to paraphrase Pogo — part of the solution, instead of part of the problem.

The second topic, I confess, is a large part of the reason I like to go cruising: the *food*. Through experience and the proliferation of modern cooking gear developed for backpackers, I am no longer compelled to wolf down cold Dinty Moore. With a little planning and a spirit of inventiveness, we can now serve up gourmet feasts in the wild — be they from foraged delicacies or from simple packaged goods artfully combined.

Now throw into the beachcruising equation your own particular interests — birdwatching, hiking, fishing, sketching, or just contemplating the beauty of it all — and you have a whole new world to discover, without high boat mortgages, marine slip rentals, storage and yard bills, crowded anchorages, or advance reservations. Your gear is all stowed for a moment's notice; just throw in the fresh stuff and go. The caveats have to do with practical matters; the style is your own.

CHAPTER One

The Boats

There is nothing—absolutely nothing—half so much worth doing as messing about in boats," said Ratty to Mole in Kenneth Grahame's *The Wind in the Willows*. This quote has become ubiquitous in the world of small boats, but it is noteworthy that Ratty, while rhapsodizing about boats in general, was given a very particular boat by his illustrator, Arthur Rackham. Since Ratty lived on the Thames River in England, it was only natural that he "mess about" in a Thames River sculling boat—a boat designed (or evolved) to suit a particular environment. There is a charming model of this boat, complete with a hand-carved Ratty and Mole aboard, on display at Mystic Seaport Museum in Connecticut, along with dozens of full-size examples of small craft of both working and pleasure boat heritage. Browsing through this collection one might wonder why there are so many different types—some flat bottomed, some round; some look heavy and clumsy, while others appear light and graceful. Aesthetics aside, the primary difference is in how and where a boat will be used: Is it for fishing, transportation, or recreation? Will it be sailed on shallow, sheltered lakes? Deep, open water?

Although the very nature of beachcruising seems to dictate a shoal-

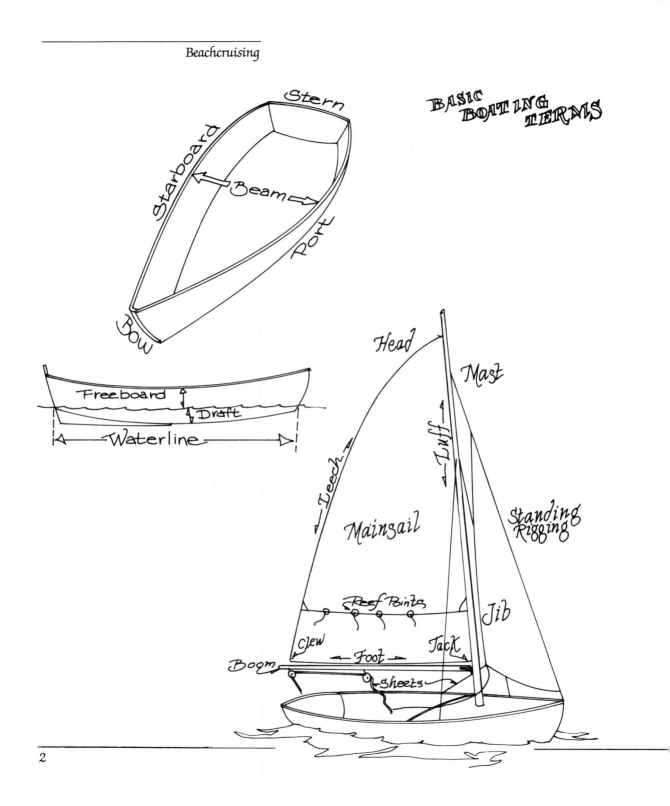

BASIC BOATING TERMS

Stern

Starboard

Beam

Port

Bow

Freeboard

Draft

Waterline

Head

Mast

Luff

Leech

Standing Rigging

Mainsail

Reef Points

Jib

Clew

Tack

Boom

Foot

Sheets

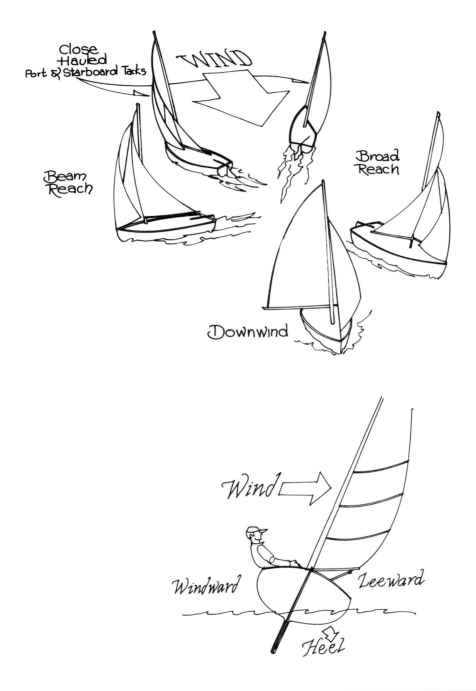

Close
Hauled
Port & Starboard Tacks

WIND

Beam
Reach

Broad
Reach

Downwind

Wind

Windward

Leeward

Heel

draft boat under 25 feet, uncomplicated in design and detail, a wide array of available watercraft fit the description. In this chapter we will establish criteria for selecting a boat tailored to your needs, as well as review some specific examples of each general type. But since most of the small craft on the recreational market today have their roots in traditional boats, it might be entertaining as well as informative to examine their history briefly.

Tradition

Life was hard in the coastal fishing communities of 18th-century America. There were few, if any, recreational watercraft. Boats were working tools—like hay wagons, sawmills, and graineries. To make a living, fishermen needed to go out every day in all kinds of weather, not just when it was pleasant. Fishing boats, regardless of size, had to be seaworthy and provide a spacious, stable working platform. A wide array of boats evolved to fill the needs of different types of fishermen, fishing in different waters for different types of fish.

One of the oldest known types of working small boat is the dory—a boat of simple, rugged construction with a particularly pretty shape. This shape evolved less from aesthetics than from need: dories were low in the middle to ease working over the side, and higher on the ends to keep out the sea. Generally about 15 to 20 feet long (dories were always measured on their bottoms; a 15-foot dory might be 20 feet long overall), they were heavy and took a good arm to row. This didn't matter, though, because dories were transported to the fishing grounds on the decks of schooners and lowered over the side to set their cod trawls—long, many-hooked lines; they didn't have to travel far on their own. Dories were extremely seaworthy when full of fish, but the wide flaring sides and narrow bottom tended to make them decidedly less so when empty. The object, however, was to fill the dory with heavy codfish. Given that, the design made sense.

Some dories had a small sprit rig for sailing downwind, and today there are devoted dory sailors who have learned the skills of using these traditional boats for cruising—enjoying a sense of connection with history along the way. But in my view, the traditional Grand Banks dory is not the handiest of recreational boats for the average user. Never intended as a sailboat—even with a modern rig it does not go to weather well—it requires experience (and a strong back) to row effectively. Still, dories are noteworthy because they were the forerunners of several variations developed for coastal waters—such as the Amesbury and Swampscott types. Still flat-bottomed and similar in beam and profile, these two boats had rounder sides, producing a fuller hull with greater initial stability. Fitted with centerboards and better rigs, they made capable sailers. Originally they were used for fishing in the waters around Gloucester, Massachusetts in the late 1800s, but the "landed gentry" who summered up that way took to these refined fishing craft and added an outlandish rig that made them very fast. The Swampscott sailing dory races are legendary—and still being run today.

Gloucester also was home to the legendary Howard Blackburn—the survivor of an incredible 60-mile row to safety after his dory went astray from its schooner in the winter of 1883. Not only did he make the Newfoundland coast (minus some frostbitten fingers and toes), but he went on to accomplish several Atlantic crossings in very small boats—though none were dories. There seems to be a fascination with setting records for traveling the farthest distance in the smallest possible boat. While some have met with tragedy, a remarkable number have succeeded—and proved to us, in the comfort of our favorite reading chair, that small boats can indeed be extraordinarily seaworthy. These vessels are not beachcruisers, of course, but specially designed sailing capsules that carry sufficient supplies to keep the skipper fed for the months it takes to cross an ocean in a 10-foot boat.

More appropriate to beachcruising, and yet another example that there is nothing new under the sun, is the 1876 cruise of the *Centennial Republic*. Nathaniel Bishop, a renowned small-boat enthusiast of the day, recognized the seaworthiness and cruising potential of another working

Amesbury Dory

Centennial Republic

boat—the Barnegat Bay Sneakbox. Looking a little like a giant watermelon seed, this flat boat was used for waterfowl hunting as well as general transportation in the marshes and waterways of the New Jersey coast, and sails and rows very well. Bishop had one built and sailed and rowed it 2,600 miles from Pittsburgh to Cedar Key on the west coast of Florida. Camping in the boat along the way, he kept a fine journal of his adventures (*Four Months in a Sneakbox,* published in 1879) and passed along valuable advice—advice that is central to beachcruising still: planning.

The small (12 feet) sneakbox allowed little room for household goods. Although he fished and provisioned along the way, Bishop had to plan his gear carefully—and there were no specialty backpacking shops to fill his needs back then: light, efficient camping gear was nearly a century in the future. Still, Bishop understood the concept, and if his trip was a bit more ambitious than most of ours, he proved it was not only possible but downright enjoyable to travel this way. It must have been, because it inspired another small boat aficionado, Christopher Cunningham, to repeat the adventure in 1985—this time in a cold-molded version of Bishop's boat, complete with modern, high-tech backpacking gear.

Another example of a traditional fishing craft that has proved popular in its recreational incarnation is the Cape Cod catboat. Its large single sail and wide, shallow-draft hull evolved because the waters of the Cape are "thin," and the winds often are light in summer. Because crews had to be paid, boats usually fished with just the skipper aboard, or with perhaps one paid hand, and the boat had to be stable and self-tending when fishing. Consequently there is a lot of room in a catboat—good for cruising; their simple rigs are easy to handle, and you can practically sail it right up on the beach. Naturally, you don't have to sail a catboat exclusively in Cape Cod. Thin water and light winds are found nearly everywhere.

At the same time the catboat was working Nantucket Sound, a little farther down the coast another fishing boat was developing. To work the oyster beds in Long Island Sound, watermen needed a shallow-draft boat that was big enough to carry a large load and fast enough—this was before the widespread use of ice to keep the catch fresh—to get the catch quickly to market. The New Haven Oyster Sharpies were impressive boats—long, graceful, and fleet; they were also very simply built. Unlike the catboats, which had a complex curved hull that required a competent shipwright to plank, the flat-bottomed, flat-sided sharpies were often built by the fishermen themselves. This very appealing design has "trick-

7

19th Century Working Catboat

led down" to quite a few modern cruisers and daysailers today—as we will see shortly.

With the advent of reliable inboard power, many small working craft, their owners in search of a competitive edge, began to mount engines. But sailing vessels do not perform well at the higher speeds made possible by power, and completely new boats developed, such as the Maine Lobsterboat, to use this new source of locomotion. From these early powerboats have evolved the current crop of efficient, small outboard boats, many of which make excellent beachcruisers. And the engines themselves have evolved. Outboard motors once had a well deserved reputation for being heavy, noisy, smelly, and cantankerous. In contrast, the newest generation of small outboards is nearly as quiet and reliable as a digital watch.

In these examples we have seen how working craft evolve and are adapted for recreational purposes. Many others have led similar lives, and since they tend to be localized there may be one indigenous to your home cruising grounds. Of course, given the mobility a simple trailer towed behind even the most compact of cars gives the small boater, an indigenous craft need hardly be limited to its native waters.

While the boats of our traditional maritime heritage were built of wood by necessity, the advent of fiberglass (and to some extent aluminum) radically changed the world of small boats. As our society industrialized, the traditional wooden boatbuilding skills, and the time available

Maine Lobsterboat
1900's Hampton

to build traditional wooden boats, diminished. And with a growing market for recreational watercraft, the few remaining active shops could not begin to fill the need.

By the late 1950s, fiberglass boats were being hailed as the greatest bonanza to boating since the discovery that wood floated. The headlong rush to market by manufacturers whose advertising departments were more talented than their designers produced some pretty God-awful boats. Since glass could be molded into about any shape imaginable, a lot of traditional design wisdom went out the window. OPEC was not a factor then, resin was cheap, and the result was a vast array of big family cruisers available for very little money. Naturally, time and some financial "tides" leveled things out—the poorer designs fell by the wayside, and even one of best, the Pearson Triton, which you could have bought for $5,000 in 1960, now costs $50,000. But for the small-boat market, fiberglass has been a boon—it means more good, affordable boats available to a larger public. Many look more like intergalactic probes than boats; others are tasteful re-creations of traditional designs.

Happily, the wooden boat industry has made a small comeback. With more dollars available for leisure activities, some boaters are willing to go the extra expense for the aesthetic pleasure of owning a well-crafted wooden boat. Provided it is a small one, the traditionally onerous chore of maintaining a wooden boat becomes bearable. But even on larger wooden boats ways have been found to minimize maintenance. One side benefit of the "plastic" revolution is the use of quality resins and glues to seal and even assemble wooden boats, eliminating their traditional weaknesses—age and rot.

Choices

There are a lot of choices out there: modern or traditional, sail or power, wood or fiberglass or aluminum. But in thinking about what boat is right for you, the first thing you should consider is not the size, shape, type, or cost of your vessel. Before you go off to boat shows, boat yards, or start poring over the classifieds, focus on the *activity,* not the vehicle. The right boat is a critical part of the success and pleasure of beachcruising, but your expectations and motivations will determine what sort of boat you ultimately use. Your own subjective relationship with the marine environment, the benefits you receive from participation, and the time you have to spend messing about in boats are the determining factors.

Paradoxically, much of this book deals with tangibles like boats, gear, food, and navigation, but all that is supportive to the experience. By learning what works, what is suitable to your own needs, and how to pare it down to exclude the things you don't need, you get closer to your purpose—however you choose to experience or interpret it.

I've often thought that harbor seals are the most natural beach-cruisers around. They need no equipment to "sail," food is acquired en route, and they can haul out on any beach they choose. I'm not going to join the debate as to who has the grander appreciation of nature, but focusing on the simplicity and freedom of the seal's "cruising" helps my own perspective.

Focusing on your own needs might help you set criteria that will help with very practical matters, such as choosing the right boat. Are you a fisherman who enjoys going out in your aluminum skiff for an afternoon, but have begun to desire not only to go farther afield but to share the experience with your family, not all of whom are fishermen? A skiff is not the only boat you can fish from. Perhaps a slightly larger, more commodious powerboat would be more appropriate—or even a shallow-draft sailboat, one with room for family and camping gear: the kids could go exploring ashore near a new fishing spot while you troll or flycast. You may find your interests changing, evolving, as the boat becomes a center for family experiences.

Maybe you have been a marina cruiser for years—trading up to bigger and bigger boats as your income (and self-image) grew. Now you have to store, maintain, and pay for that 30-footer. Instead of the dreams of

peace, solitude, and far tropical isles, your weekends seem filled with un-invited guests, crowded marinas or anchorages, anxious monitoring of weather forecasts, and bills. Is this why you bought the big boat? Sell it! Buy something too small for guests, launch it off a trailer, take a day cruise or an overnight or week—anytime the mood strikes. Have enough dry goods and gear always on board so you can pack the cooler and be off in an hour. Put the money you used to pay the marina and the boatyard and the chandlery and the finance company toward early retirement.

Think of it: You are still out there on the same water as you were before, only now you can get close enough to the roses to smell them—in this case the wonderful wild ones that grow on remote beaches. If you still, now and then, lust for a week aboard the "big one," with its hot showers, cushy berths, full galley, and air-conditioning, charter it. You pays your money, you has your fun, and you deliver it back to the owner to worry about. Meanwhile, your own little beachcruiser sits ready (and paid for) on the trailer behind the house.

It's considered mean in yachting circles to dwell overmuch on cost, but cost is a legitimate consideration, and we're not really talking about yachting. Beachcruising is by definition the opposite of the go-now-pay-later way we tend to approach some of our "needs." Whether you can af-ford it isn't the issue; the kind of boating we are talking about hardly rates as conspicuous consumption. On the bottom of the scale you can go beachcruising for under $2,000; on the other end of the scale you'd be hard pressed to spend over $20,000. The boats I have spent the least on

were the ones I used the most. To put it another way, to justify a $50,000 cruiser you'd have to spend about every day for the next five years aboard. Here's how it breaks down:

A $50,000 boat (actually a pretty modest vessel by today's standards) financed over 10 years will cost you about $445 per month. Figure an additional $500 per year for insurance; $500 (minimum) for maintenance and yard bills; and another $500 or so for slip rental. There's $6,840 per year (assuming nothing major goes wrong—like needing a new $1,200 mainsail, or a new $4,500 engine) year in, year out. If you're like most boaters, the realities of regular jobs and other demands for your time will mean you'll use your big boat on eight summer weekends and for your two-week vacation. At *best*, 30 days of boating, at $228 per day.

I don't deny that the ownership of luxury has its good points—after all, everything is relative. But take a good look at where your dollars are going, and how much you have to pay for your freedom.

Suppose your interest is in cruising, but as yet you've not been aboard anything bigger than a Sunfish, if that. I'd not suggest that you pack your gear and head down the coast in whatever the salesman who saw you coming put you into. But looking at it another way, you have the pleasure of entering a new activity without prejudice—and if you exercise a little prudence you have a whole new world ahead of you. Though being on the water has to be done with reasonable respect for the elements, it ain't necessarily so that you have to be born with salt water in your veins to be good at it. You can start slowly, perhaps go with friends who have experience; take some lessons in seamanship—preferably from someone who is a real teacher, not a self-proclaimed "salt" who takes you under his wing only to point out your ignorance of the fine points of seafaring.

For some, boating is the whole experience—just being out on the water is enough; what they see along the way is incidental, though I suspect there are few who aren't inspired by the beauty before them, unless they are whizzing by it at 50 miles per hour in a candyflake-red Donzi. I think in truth we are a bit of all of the foregoing, the question remains as to what our particular motivations and interests really are—and that, though it may seem a long way from Mr. Bishop and his sneakbox—is how we get to the boat.

If you have begun to formulate your list of interests, the process of choosing a boat begins with determining whether it's seawothy and whether it's to be oar-, sail-, or outboard-powered.

Seaworthiness applies to *all* boats, and though we will look at a wide range of watercraft designed for various conditions and uses, a buyer's guide to a safe and sound boat is the most appropriate place to begin your search. Essentially two factors determine seaworthiness: design and construction. Design is tied to use and the prevailing local conditions. A boat that is more than adequate on a river, lake, or in a protected bay may be utterly helpless in offshore coastal conditions.

A comprehensive treatise on boat design isn't reasonable here—though you might find it interesting to read some of the books on the subject. You should determine where you intend to cruise, and then using the reviews in this book or from other references, find out what types of boats are most suitable for that kind of waterway. Add your own requirements on size, motive power, and cost. The reviews of the various categories that follow should give you a good idea of which boat will best suit your needs.

It would be no more appropriate to try to sail a shoal-draft pocket cruiser across the Bay of Fundy (with its 20-foot tides) than to try to negotiate a small river with a fly-bridge offshore sportfisherman.

You might begin by making a list something like this:

1. Type of power
   a. Sail?
   b. Outboard?
   c. Rowing?
2. Range
   a. Local, protected waterways?
   b. Larger lakes, bays, coastal islands?
   c. Extended coastal or river cruising?
3. Size
   a. How many people (usually)?
   b. Length of use (day; weekend; longer)?
4. Accommodation
   a. Open day boat?
   b. Cuddy cabin overnighter?

Once you determine the type or design that fits your needs and wallet, the next factor to consider is construction. Since most boats are built of fiberglass today, let's look at some of the construction methods used in that industry. The easiest and least expensive way to produce a boat is with a sprayed "chop"—a mixture of resin and chopped glass fibers sprayed from an air-powered gun into a mold. This works perfectly well for small dinghies and rowboats, but it is hard to control hull thickness, and there is no particular directional stability. Unless chop is combined with another means of stiffening or strengthening the hull, it is not especially appropriate for boats much over 10 or 12 feet.

The next method is called hand layup: A skin of gelcoat (the shiny outside of a glass boat) is sprayed on the female mold, followed by various layers of fiberglass cloth, matt (chopped fiber pressed into a loose, thick blanket) and sometimes a heavier, burlap-type glass cloth called roving. Glass cloth may be used alone, or it may be combined with the stronger, more sophisticated (and more expensive) carbon fiber materials.

Today, a lot of fiberglass boats are built with an inner core of balsa or foam—for lighter weight and greater stiffness. This type of construction is especially suitable for larger boats with broad, fairly flat surfaces. Single-skin fiberglass is strong when curved, but quite weak when flat. Quality of each type can vary, but one way to judge a fiberglass boat is to sight along the outside of the hull. If it appears excessively wavy it means that the mold was never properly faired out, and since the mold is the major investment in the tooling process a cheap job here usually means cheap production all the way down the line.

Today's fiberglass industry has developed some high standards of quality, and though it is unregulated, the insurance companies have helped establish guidelines—for obvious reasons. In new boats you can examine the workmanship visually.

Older used boats must be examined more critically. Contrary to myth, fiberglass is not indestructible, and is vulnerable not only to abrasion, impact, and stress, but its chemistry eventually begins to break down from prolonged exposure to ultraviolet rays if not properly protected. Look for crazing, cracks, or stress fractures, both inside and outside the hull. Sometimes the gelcoat looks dulled, but that does not mean the boat is weak: gelcoat oxidizes, but it can usually be renewed—either with special polishes or with new gelcoat or paint.

If the boat you are considering is of 1970s vintage, be especially vigilant—not only for signs of age, but for cheap construction. Because it was a boom time for the boating industry, some boats were built with borderline construction methods. I remember one big yellow-hulled sailboat advertised to "sleep five" in 22 feet. Pushing against the side of the hull, I was startled to see it "oilcan"—and I'm no Arnold Schwarzenegger. Climbing inside past the gaudy velour cushions and pile carpeting, I could see light coming through the thin fiberglass hull. The company that built them is no longer in business, but those boats are still out there. Beware.

Fittings, fastenings, and running gear should be carefully examined.

Good hardware is expensive, but cheap hardware can be even more costly if it fails at the wrong time. Fittings should be rust*proof*, not rust resistant. Stainless steel, bronze, and anodized aluminum are the best materials. Deck hardware that will be under strain should be backed on the underside with metal plates or wood cleats: fiberglass can rupture under stress if not reinforced. Hardware should also be bedded with silicone or another waterproof sealer; contrary to popular belief, fiberglass can "rot."

These are just some basic guidelines; you can learn a lot more from some excellent boat buying and surveying guides on the market. I'm not suggesting you have to become an expert to buy a boat. Quality feels like quality, and that is the ultimate test. If you're looking at a boat with a lot of rough edges, loose or too-small hardware, unfinished surfaces, cheap trim, or parts that don't fit, be skeptical. And above all, if you don't understand a feature the salesman is touting, ask what he means. It's not against the rules to admit unfamiliarity with some esoteric aspect of a boat; boats are full of mysterious stuff anyhow—most of which is just doggerel for some plain function.

Other than Ratty and his Thames scull, the best-known fictional small boat (for those over 35 who remember Walt Kelly's comic strip) was Pogo's Okefenokee Swamp Scow. Now there was a boat for the purpose. *"We wan't goin' noplace egxactly so it git there 'bout as quick as it*

need." Built, no doubt, from swamp cypress, it was flat-bottomed, square sided, and rugged—with a good pair of oars and room for ol' Albert's considerable lunch. It seemed to fulfill their needs perfectly. Despite the boat's confusion over its identity (it never had the same name twice, and frequently carried two different ones at the same time, such as The *Hon. J. Pilkington Smythe* on the stern and the *S.S. Westphalian Ham* on the side), it was safe from swamp rats, snakes, and politicians, and so it did its job.

In a small boat, the better it does the main thing, the less important become the things it does not do, or cannot do for its size. As we begin to look at specific boats, bear in mind what you want the boat to do, what it is conservatively capable of doing, and what you are prepared to do without—given that the kinds of boats we are looking at here are not floating condos.

One other, very serious consideration: FUN! If the craft in question is more work to operate than it is fun to own, something is wrong. It is either too much boat, or too little, or you had the wrong expectations of it.

Small Boat Categories

The boats in this chapter do not represent a comprehensive review of the market; rather, they are an overview of the various types available, and how they relate to beachcruising.

SEA KAYAKS

Of all the boats in this book, the sea kayak will be discussed the least—not because it is the least boat; far from it—but because it is possibly the most active class of beachcruiser today, and by that token, the most widely written about. There are books, periodicals, and probably enough experienced kayakers in your area to consult if this becomes your interest. The kayak is a fast and agile craft, capable of going to a wide range of places, but any kayaker will tell you that it is not a cruising boat for novices. Kayak touring requires training and experience.

I have friends who are avid kayakers, and I respect their approach. Kayakers tend to embody the best of attitudes toward their environment. They have also been instrumental in the development of the camping and cruising gear that must be compact enough to fit aboard the slim craft and yet make for comfortable camping once ashore. Beachcruising, at

least as described in this book, is perhaps a less muscular and more leisurely activity in general than kayaking—even though I believe all of us who take to the water in this fashion must be kindred spirits no matter what the pace or vehicle.

CANOES

I have been a sailor all of my life, and did not until recently own a canoe. I don't think I ever considered a canoe as a cruising boat—more something to paddle up the proverbial lazy river. Well, the river I live on is tidal, wide, long, and anything but lazy, yet after buying a canoe I discovered it was more than capable of travel on that waterway. Picking our weather, my son and I paddle downriver and out to a nearby coastal island for an overnighter. This particular canoe is an E.M. White (now sold by Old Town) 12-footer—beamy, light, and quite seaworthy. We were able to land and carry it ashore on a rock-bound island inaccessible to anything heavier or bigger. A canoe like that certainly is about the least expensive way to go cruising, though you have to accept, and work with, its limitations. A light, open canoe is no place to be caught out in a hard blow offshore, or even on a lake.

What is of historical interest is that canoes were virtually the first recreational touring boats in this country. In the late 1800s the American Canoe Association was formed at Lake George, New York, for the purpose of furthering interest in the canoe as a cruising vessel. It was thus the first beachcruiser, with thousands of devoted followers. Today, like the kayak, many good books and publications are on the market, as well as active associations. I'm not going to profile touring canoes here, since, like the kayak, the existing literature is already comprehensive, but I will say that the canoe makes a fine introduction to freestyle cruising—some can even be fitted with sailing rigs for extended range.

I'd like to take take a moment to acknowledge a predecessor in this notion of free-spirit boating. In 1920, *Forest and Stream* published a little book called *Woodcraft* by "Nessmuk," aka George Washington Sears. It is a witty and practical guide to camping in general, with some interesting ideas about a proper canoe for the job. In fact, Sears commissioned several, one of which weighed in at only 16 pounds. If you are a good used-book finder, Dover Books re-published it in 1963, but it ain't been seen much since then. It might be worth the search as it is a delightful read.

ROWING BOATS

For those who wish to combine fitness with cruising, there are some alternatives to canoes and kayaks that allow more room for gear and crew. With different concepts in design the following examples are both capable rowing craft, with open-water abilities.

Gypsy is a rowing/touring boat designed by the renowned small-boat designer Phil Bolger. An experienced naval architect, free thinker, and sometime-maverick designer, Bolger has addressed about every boating need at one time or another. As an amateur designer myself I'm sometimes at odds with some of his solutions—either on practical or aesthetic grounds—but he has indisputably had a strong impact on the small-boat field.

One of Bolger's best creations is this 15-foot rowing boat. With a low profile, light weight, no draft to speak of, and with enough stability to handle a variety of conditions and hold a lot of gear, *Gypsy* is an able boat for the "muscle cruiser." It also has a small sailing rig, though the very low freeboard that reduces windage when rowing makes for a rather wet boat when sailing on the wind. It tracks well; its long, pointed bow rises easily over a sea; its bottom is flat, stable, but not too wide to create excessive drag when rowing.

Gypsy is big enough for two people and 100 pounds of gear to enjoy a nice cruise, camping ashore. At 95 pounds of dry weight, you could haul it on to some normally difficult beaches. In experienced hands it can be used in open coastal waters, though short hops should be carefully planned; if the weather kicked up it would be a hard boat to maneuver safely in short choppy seas. It has some record voyages to its credit though. Some years back *Small Boat Journal* (now *Boat Journal*) carried

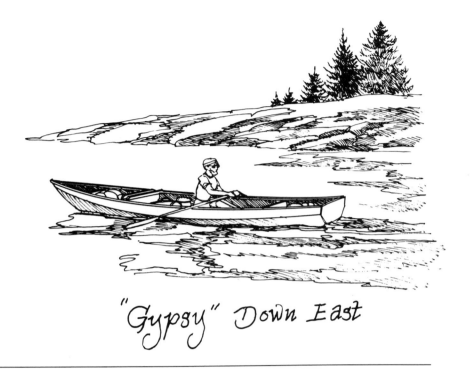

"Gypsy" Down East

an account of a long, singlehanded cruise in *Gypsy,* downeast on the rugged Maine coast.

Gypsy will cartop or trailer easily. Its only drawback is availability; there is no commercially produced version, although do-it-yourself plans are readily available. There are a fair number of boats in this category, and recent developments in the techniques of plywood and epoxy boatbuilding have simplified the work—housewives, parish priests, CEOs, even those who have never built a bookcase have successfully put together a small boat. The technique has been particularly well developed and promoted by Harold "Dynamite" Payson of South Thomaston, Maine. Not only has he built the prototypes of most of Bolger's small boats, but he has written many step-by-step articles and books on how to build them. His approach is a simple, no-nonsense method, with plenty of native wisdom and humor thrown in—just at the critical moment when you have resin stuck to your fingers on a hot humid day and are ready to burn the whole thing.

If you are not up to the challenge of building a boat yourself, or are just not interested, you can usually find a local builder who will do the job for you. But building a small cruising boat can be a singularly rewarding experience. And if you have a little spare weekend and evening time, it can save you some money.

Still in the rowing category, but from a very different perspective, is the peapod. This is a traditional design used by fishermen in coastal Maine, developed 100 years ago or more, but still in wide use today, both as a working boat and a recreational craft. It is heavier than *Gypsy*, high sided and round-bottomed. The seaworthiness of peapods is legendary. One local story tells of two lobstermen caught out in a gale in their peapod. A schooner, itself being badly thrown about by the storm, came upon the pair and offered to take them aboard. The two men declined, saying they felt safer in their sturdy little double-ender.

With a very full midsection and fine ends, a peapod moves very easily through the water despite its bulk. Underwater it is more canoe-like—its reserve buoyancy is about on the waterline where you need it. A peapod generally has a long, straight skeg, which keeps it going where you point it. It does not beach as easily as *Gypsy*, but you can anchor in shallow water or nudge it ashore on a beach. Though it will carry a good sailing rig, and is adequate for pottering along, it is not an especially fast sailer.

With a lot of interior room, you can stow plenty of cruising gear, and with some boards across the seats and a boom tent you can even sleep aboard. Some of the peapods were fitted with raised oarlocks—the Maine lobstermen rowed standing up and facing forward so they could tend their traps—and in calm waters this is an enjoyable way to row: it's nice to see where you're going, rather than where you've been.

Peapods are being built again by the new small wooden boat shops,

Matinicus Peapod

and also are available in fiberglass. Other rowing boats also available in wood or fiberglass with a long maritime heritage are the Whitehall, the Delaware Ducker, the Sneakbox, and the Rangely boat. These are all proven, seaworthy, coastwise, lake, and river boats.

Wind-powered

DAYSAILERS

For some reason, a scene played out many times in one variation or another is that of an older sailor sitting on the stern of his anchored 55-footer, or perhaps on the veranda of the yacht club, looking wistfully down upon a suntanned youth cavorting around with his gauze-stick-and-string dinghy. If there is a listener within earshot, the old salt doubtless is saying something like, "Now that's what sailing is all about. I remember when, back in. . . ." And he also remembers how he traded up from bigger boat to bigger boat, and though some of it has been a grand adventure, the experiences of one's first boat are never forgotten. Maybe the kind of sailing beachcruising should be about is a blend of the simplicity of an uncomplicated sailing skiff, with just enough creature comforts and size to extend the cruising range and satisfy the more sophisticated needs and interests of maturity.

An eight-foot dinghy might not exactly qualify as a beachcruiser, but it is possible to do some fine coastal, lake, and bay exploring in some pretty small boats. Going back to tradition for one of the oldest daysailers still around, I'd consider the Cape Cod Beetle Cat as a good start. In 1920 John Beetle, a builder of whaleboats until the decline of that industry, turned his shop at New Bedford, Massachusetts, to producing a small recreational catboat designed to teach children to sail. This 12-footer was beamy, safe, well-made (some of the first ones are still sailing), and lively enough to keep a kid's interest. Since then thousands of them have been built—virtually the same way save for the addition of bronze fittings and Dacron sails. In 1948 the Concordia Company of South Dartmouth, Massachusetts, bought the rights and continues producing them today.

Anyone who has ever been aboard a Beetle Cat will tell you that there is more sprawling room in the cockpit of this little boat than in the cockpit of some full-size cruisers. There is also enough space forward under the wide deck to stow sufficient gear for a two-week excursion, if you care to go that long without a shower. You could set up a boom tent to sleep

Beetle Cat

aboard (one is made for the boat as an option), or take your duffel and camp ashore. A little outboard would let you explore some windless rivers and backwaters—the boat only draws a few inches with the board up. With its stiff hull, the Beetle Cat has enough reserve stability to make even the novice feel secure. I think the cruising crew should be limited to two, but a family with one or two small children might manage a weekend in one.

Down in the land of perpetual sunshine, blue water, and fair winds, cruising certainly ought to be a laid-back activity. And without fog, 20-foot tides, and cold nor'easters to deal with, small open boats seem particularly appropriate. There are a couple of builders down in the Sunshine State who seem to agree with this.

Hens are well-designed, soundly built boats, dedicated to the spirit and soul of light-boat cruising. Although unlikely to win the prettiest boat in the harbor award, they are function plus pleasure personified.

The 17-foot Marsh Hen is what you might term a "convertible" open boat. It is a double ended, flat-bottomed sharpie type, with a single sail and a host of built-in places to put things. At night, a custom-fitted canvas structure makes a snug two-berth cabin, which can also be left in

23

place under sail — great for those places in the country where it really rains, or where the midday sun makes life in the cockpit unbearable.

The Marsh Hen's rig deserves attention — though its type is not unique. It is set on an unstayed aluminum mast and has a sprit boom — which fastens higher on the mast than a conventional marconi boom, and has two benefits: it keeps the clew of the sail down when sailing off the wind, and your crew doesn't have to duck when the sail comes across. Sail control is simple. In light air you ease the tension on the sprit to "balloon" the sail; in heavy air you pull it taut to flatten the cloth and reduce the air pocket. Reefing is done vertically, simply by pulling a brailing line that gathers some of the sail forward against the mast. With no jib to bring around on each tack, it is the best of easy sailing — you just point the boat where you want it to go. There is some tradeoff for this laid-back style. While the sail is ample and performs smoothly in all conditions, you could not call the speed impressive. Well-mannered would be a better description, but with the Hen's creature comforts I'd say she is one of the best of the open beach boats.

Another of Florida's active small-boat builders is Marine Concepts of Clearwater, builders of the Sea Pearl — a 21-foot, ketch-rigged, open cruiser/daysailer more akin to the peapod — though very contemporary in concept. Narrow for its length (6½-foot beam), the boat seems tender at first, but when heeled over slightly she stiffens up and slips along very smoothly — and the two sails will balance her so that you hardly have to touch the helm on a reach. Compared with the Marsh Hen, the Sea Pearl is a little more performance-oriented — and perhaps a little better-suited to longer trips. At 550 pounds (dry weight), she is actually lighter than the Marsh Hen, though there is not nearly the room in her. The deck is recessed all around, providing plenty of good places to sit, and the boat is open under the deck for ample stowage. There is a snug-fitting pram hood over the cockpit well that allows sufficient sleeping room for one, but it would be tight for two. As a solo cruiser it is self-contained — in fact a Sea Pearl has done the Intracoastal Waterway in that fashion — but for a crew it would be better-suited to camping ashore.

Lateral resistance is provided by a leeboard mounted on a pivot on either side of the boat. Several small boats use this device — it allows more room in the center of the boat than a centerboard, and does not require a complicated, watertight trunk. Leeboards take a little getting used to, but they are effective, economical, and require a minimum of maintenance. The wishbone rig — a variation of the spritsail — is easy to use; reefing can be accomplished quickly by simply rolling up the mizzen.

Both of these boats were designed to accommodate the dual func-

Marsh Hen

tions of daysailing and open-boat cruising. Consideration was given to stowage, alternate propulsion (oarlocks and outboard brackets), and a performance range capable of handling a reasonable array of weather likely to be encountered on a short cruise. They are both sold equipped for basic cruising—the needed additions being cooking, navigation, and safety gear.

Far from the sparkling waters of Biscayne Bay are the less-than-hospitable sailing grounds off the English coast. Yet intrepid fishermen have plied those waters for centuries—in tough, no-nonsense, open boats. Out of that heritage has come the Drascombe line of recreational sailboats, with models ranging from 15 to 21 feet. The common denominator in the Drascombe family is hull shape. Flat on the bottom, with several lapped chines, a very full, stiff midsection, with the fullness carried well to the ends, the Drascombe hull yields a buoyant boat able to ride high in a seaway.

The rig is a low-aspect yawl, loose-footed, but ample to power the

Drascombe Lugger

boat along without much danger of capsizing in a sudden gust. Drascombe boats are so well balanced that they will sail themselves for long periods while the skipper tends to lunch, reading, or navigation. The interior has several watertight lockers, and seating all around on the recessed deck. Sleeping aboard the larger models is possible, on the floor between the side seats, and tents are available. These are tough little cruisers, very British—salty-looking and capable—so much so that one intrepid sailor, Webb Chiles, has sailed his Drascombe Longboat nearly around the world, documenting his adventures in *Cruising World* magazine. It is fascinating reading, complete with shipwrecks, pirates—the works; but if you are just tentatively dabbling an exploratory toe into this boating activity perhaps it is not the first thing you should read. The Drascombe boats are well-built in fiberglass; a few are still available in glued-lap marine plywood if you want to feel more traditional.

Another English boat, with a similar hull form but of a more modern, sloop-rigged design, is the Wayfarer Dinghy. Don't let the word dinghy mislead you; this is a 16-footer with a record of North Sea voyages as impressive as the Drascombe. Small-boat cruising pioneers Frank and Margaret Dye have been sailing one for many years, though in a fashion a bit more adventuresome than most of us care to experience. Still, since what we are talking about in this book is choices, in their case they have chosen to trade some hardships at sea for the rewards of a very independent style of cruising.

The Wayfarer is a fast boat, and though it is decked forward and along the sides, it can be very wet in a chop to windward—gear must be stowed in waterproof bags. It is a little cramped for sleeping, too, since there is a large centerboard trunk in the middle. Its central virtue remains its extraordinary sailing ability, in nearly all weather. The Wayfarer is available in kit form for those who wish to build one, or used ones can often be found on the market.

The four boats reviewed thus far are well-designed for cruising and are ready, for the most part, to take adventuring. You can see the range— from the docile, poke-along type to the lets-see-if-we-can-sail-to-Newfoundland variety (it's been done)—which is not to say that the latter can't be used for the former.

Except on the used-boat market, none of the above is available for less than $5,000, and by the time you add a trailer and other options, considerably more. Still, this is a reasonable investment, well below most compact cars, and a lot more fun—and less than half the down payment on a real cabin cruiser. However, if your budget is more limited than that, or if you are just starting out and don't really know what boat will be right for you, you can look over the field of pure daysailers—with an eye to adapting one for a modest cruiser.

We saw earlier how the Beetle Cat could be used; a wide array of contemporary and traditional open boats could be similarly adapted. As an example, O'Day has been making a range of boats from 12 to 17 feet for a long time; they are affordable either new or used. Of course choosing a small, light daysailer will mean your cruising area cannot be as ambitious as it might be with a larger, better equipped boat. Nevertheless, a converted daysailer, in many waters, will get you going. The important features to look for in a daysailer you intend to convert to a beachcruiser are solid construction, ample freeboard and beam, under-deck stowage (completely open boats with no flotation would be a risky choice), and a rig that can be easily controlled, reefed, and set up.

Next you need to think about how to modify your day boat for cruising. Just imagine loading up your nice comfortable sloop with camping gear and a cooler of good food, setting off down the coast, or up the lake toward a little island. The sun is warm, the breeze just right, and off you go. Around 11 o'clock though, it's getting windier and there are clouds building to the east. Normally you'd just turn around and head home, right? Except that you're cruising, and you really want to get to that island. So maybe you put a reef in the sail and keep going. The sailing gets tougher, but still it's not too bad, except that the spray keeps coming aboard, soaking you, your gear, and your tuna-and-avocado sandwiches. By the time you do reach that island you are wet, cranky, and there's still camp to make—and it looks like rain. Some cruise—maybe you should have stuck to daysailing.

Not necessarily. Most small cruising boats are designed to keep the water out, at least most of it, and usually there are lockers to stow gear. Daysailers, on the other hand, usually have little dry storage space, and do little toward keeping the crew dry. With a little extra gear and some small modifications, however, you can correct much of that. The first, and most involved, would be to make, or have made, a small dodger to fit forward—abaft the mast but wide and high enough to keep the spray out of the cockpit and provide a place for keeping gear dry, even a spot to duck under in the event of a squall. A good canvas shop can help you with this, or you could do it yourself by looking at the commercially available ones for other boats or following the instructions in one of the books listed in the bibliography. Having decided on a dodger, however, you will probably need to rearrange the sail controls, especially halyards, so that they run through blocks at the base of the mast and aft to cleats in the cockpit. This is a good idea anyway, since small daysailers rarely pro-

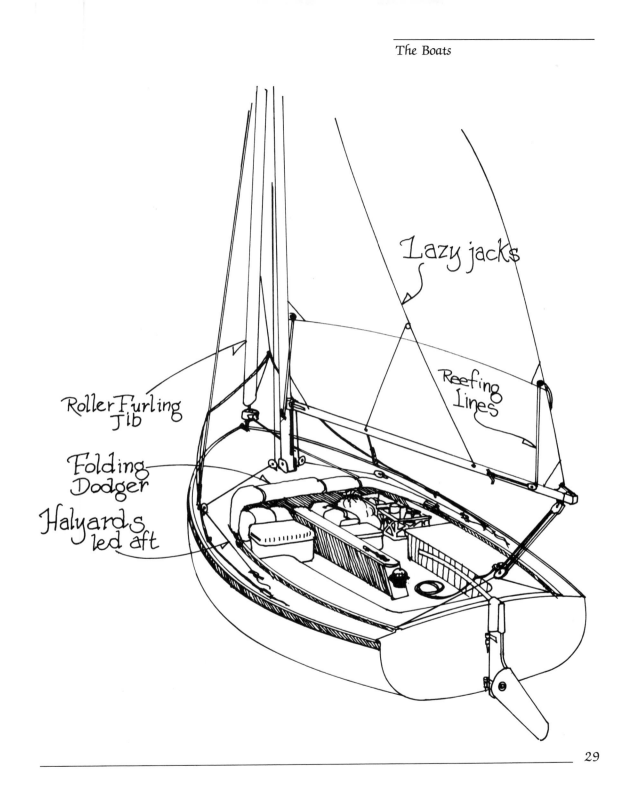

Lazy jacks

Reefing lines

Roller Furling Jib

Folding Dodger

Halyards led aft

vide a stable platform in rough conditions for crawling out on deck to lower sails. Try to plan everything to be within reach of the cockpit. This might also mean considering a furling jib—not inexpensive, but very convenient, not to mention a safe way of controlling sails.

In addition to keeping dry, you will need to beef up your navigation and safety gear—though the specifics will be covered in their respective sections. What is important is that simple, well-thought-out modifications can turn a daysailer into a modest cruiser—and some fine beachcruising can be had for a reasonable investment. For some it may even be the perfect, ultimate solution. You'll find additional ideas for refining your cruiser in Chapter 2.

I'd like to return for a moment to the kid with his backside hanging out over the weather rail, the tiller hauled up under his chin, and a grin on his face as be careens recklessly (or so it seems) toward the dock. He'll probably round up at just the right moment and step casually out in front of his peers—or he might misjudge and wind up in the drink—but he is having a grand time and learning to be a confident sailor. A simple boat, well rigged, can make a happy, confident cruiser out of you if you approach it with the right attitude. If your sailing expectations aren't too high and you respect what your boat can and cannot do, you will step out of it some fine evening onto a warm beach, far from the madding crowd, and bask peacefully in the glow of the setting sun.

SEMI-ENCLOSED CUDDY CABIN CRUISERS

These boats are not, or at least they should not, be daysailers with cabins pasted on. A responsible designer knows how the craft he has on the drawing board will be used and designs accordingly. Yet even a small cabin sloop need not be a complicated affair. There are some "miniature yachts" out there to be sure, and they may be appealing in the brochures or in the showroom; just bear in mind that many are designed to appeal to what is familiar—the comforts of home—except few of us live in 18-foot houses. This is not to say that some pocket cruisers are not thoughtfully designed, it's just that you have to re-scale your thinking.

For instance, consider the typical 18- to 20-footer advertised as sleeping four, plus a built-in head and galley. Now try to imagine four of you stuck in there all afternoon in a rainy, fogbound, hot and humid backwater. Then measure the berth widths, and compare them with your bed at home. Now imagine performing household chores in there, or moving your gear around with everyone else in the way. And if the cabin is "large" for the length, what about the cockpit, where you spend most of your time anyway? You can't put a quart in a pint pot. If the cabin is large, obviously the cockpit is short.

Before I bring the wrath of pocket cruiser builders down on my head, let me say that if you consider limiting your crew, being flexible in your needs, and don't plan on a month-long sojourn with the whole family, these boats can be perfectly suitable, although for beachcruisers they're crowding the high end of cost, though still well below "yachts." Were I to take a position against them it would be to undermine the premise of what I espouse — the freedom of personal style. Most of the activities described in this book can be done in a fairly wide variety of watercraft — my limitations are tied to a balance of cost, simplicity, and ease of operation.

If you begin by thinking of the cuddy cabin, or semi-enclosed type of cruiser as having a dry, secure place for your gear, a place to get out of the weather, and a place to sleep if you choose to stay aboard, then you will be able to get the most out of one. Let's begin with one of the smallest, though most popular of cuddy-cabin sailboats. Developed first in England in the 1950s as a plywood boat, the West Wight Potter is now built in fiberglass by HMS Marine of Marina del Rey, California. As if to reprove the theory that small boats, very small boats, can safely (if slowly) make long ocean passages, intrepid Potterers have recorded crossings from Mexico to Hawaii, across the North Sea, and from New York to Key West! Not what you'd call beachcruising exactly, but remarkable for a boat that is 15 feet long overall, $5\frac{1}{2}$ feet on the beam, weighs 500 pounds dry, and does not have what you'd call a towering sail plan. What it does have is a well-thought-out design: a slight vee bottom with a sharp forefoot to cut through waves, a hard chine for maximum stability, and a balanced rig sufficient to drive the boat's light-displacement hull, but not enough to overpower it.

Balance is more important than sail area. Even if a small boat were stiff enough to carry a very large sailplan it would be much like putting a 30-h.p. outboard on a small dinghy; the boat would drown in its own waves. As a general rule, a sailboat's potential speed — its hull speed — is the square root of the waterline expressed in nautical miles per hour. Thus in the case of the Potter, with a length of 12 feet, the designed speed is 3.46 knots. This is not to say that a boat cannot sail faster than that — wind speed, current, type of rig, etc. are all factors that control speed — but it is safe to say that waterline length gives a reasonable estimate of average speed. Speed in small boats is a relative factor anyway, since the whole range is well within that of a good jogger. In the end, the qualities

West Wight Potter

that make a good all-round sailer are the ability to point high, track well, and handle a variety of conditions.

Although the Potter may be modest in flat-out speed, her design enables her to sail near her maximum speed under most conditions in relative safety and comfort. By comparison, a fast open centerboarder of the same length may plane at six knots, but be so light and tender that it will capsize easily when it breezes up. And the very qualities that make it tack and accelerate quickly may diminish its ability to maintain a safe and steady course in a blow.

The Potter has many devoted and long-standing owners who appreciate the boat's abilities and who have learned to adapt to her limited accommodations. The cabin is minimal—ideal for one, chummy for two—but if you think of it as a sort of fiberglass pup tent it is reasonably comfortable to sleep in, with the rest of the cruising functions being carried out in the cockpit. The Potter is trailerable behind even the smallest of cars, thus having its cruising range extended in limitless directions.

Larry Brown is the undisputed champion of the Potter, and his *Sailing America* (International Marine, 1990) is an account, well worth reading, of his travels, adventures, and modifications of this well-built and by now legendary little "ship."

The largest boat in our survey is another of Phil Bolger's designs—the Dovekie, build by Edey and Duff in Mattapoiset, Massachusetts. While essentially a big double-ended sharpie, it is the most radical boat in this book. Neither truly a cabin boat nor an open one, it is completely open from stem to stern below "decks," but as you can see by the drawing it has an unusual shape. All to a purpose though: the open hatches (though they have covers) are for working the rig; the "roll bar" acts as a boom crutch and a place to fasten the canvas "after cabin." Inside there are benches, spaces for gear, and still other spaces to sleep, though the layout is informal and up to you. When the wind is light or nonexistent, you can row by sticking your long sweeps out the two rowing ports; you peer up through the after hatch to see where you are going—or more properly where you've been. The boat rows surprisingly well, which is due to the fact that even though it is 21 1/2 feet long it weighs only 600 pounds!

Lateral resistance is provided by very large leeboards, which may be locked in place from inside the boat; despite their ungainly appearance, they work very well. The rig is a single sprit mast raked aft, set with stays. To my way of thinking it could use a small jib, but as compensation there is a little "bow board" up forward that can be used to help a windward course, especially in the shallows this boat lives to explore (it draws only 4 inches with the leeboards up; maybe 5 1/2 inches with your St. Bernard along). If you own one you probably have to endure some stares and the odd derisive comment, but Dovekie has a strong following.

Using the criteria we've established thus far I'd say she's a highly qualified beachcruiser—and could handle a family with ease. A good sailor could keep her going through some pretty nasty weather, though with her light weight she gets her rail down fast; early reefing is a must. Construction is sound, but not fancy—some rough interior surfaces are evident—but for her size she's not very expensive, and you could fancy her up if you had the time or inclination. Obviously she will trailer, probably behind a Volkswagen Beetle—which in her efficiency and eccentric design she is related to.

My favorite classical music radio host gets to play his own favorites once a year on his birthday. Since this is my book I get to pick a favorite of my own, without apologizing. My recent purchase of *White Heron*—a 16-foot fiberglass keel sloop—was as much of a surprise to my wife and

DOVKIE

"White Heron"
Capri 16

me as it was to the many who know me as a long-standing wooden boat fan, shoal draft extremist, sharpie designer, builder, and cruiser.

Without taking one moment away from the pleasures I've had over the years aboard my little Nantucket and Maine Sharpies, I had arrived at a point, perhaps without knowing it, where I wanted a boat capable of a little better performance.

I was spoiled by the simplicity of the sharpies, but that simplicity rarely translated into larger boats. Then I chanced by a local yacht broker's yard and saw a simple but appealing 16-footer sitting in a cradle. Somehow the unconscious computer that had been absorbing boat specs for years went off, and I nodded to myself that this one felt "right"—until I looked underneath and saw that it had a keel, with wings no less! "Oh no," I thought, "the marketing boys have really been at this one!" I had been in Newport the year the Aussies took home *THE CUP* and had seen the miracle keel, and ever since that famous appendage has been appearing on every other conceivable boat. In this case I assumed it would have about as much effect as a spoiler on a Volkswagen. Champion of the shoal-draft beach boat that I am, I as much told the dealer so, but he just shrugged and offered to let my try one.

I've been preaching freedom of choice in this book, but I was caught with my prejudices in place. No, I cannot beach the boat, but at $2^1/_2$ feet of draft I can get close enough to make rowing ashore in the inflatable a simple alternative. That out of the way, I shall make the story somewhat shorter: We took delivery of the Capri 16 (built by Catalina) and sailed her the 40 miles home—starting against a gusty sou'wester and encompassing just about every combination of wind and sea Maine has to offer, including ghosting home in the early evening in a nearly flat calm. Simply put, it works, and does so under a wide variety of conditions. The wing keel dampens the pitching common to small boats, it digs in its determined fins to lift you to windward, and combined with the boat's beamy (6-foot, 11-inch), stiff hull, a modern rig with solid-stay jib furling, and cunningham, vang, and jiffy reef as standard equipment—well it just feels and behaves like a larger boat.

Yet I want to emphasize that despite its high-tech pedigree, it remains a simple, straightforward, well-crafted boat—it has nothing it doesn't need. There is a cuddy cabin with two comfortable, wide berths; a long cockpit with good back and foot support; and enough stability for one to walk around the entire rail without tipping the boat more than two or three inches. Thus I make my case for its inclusion, as it meets many of the criteria we've established—and offers some of the nicer features of larger performance and cruising boats—yet at a price within range of the others. It is trailerable, though you need a steeper ramp than for a center- or leeboard boat, and at 1,400 pounds, probably a bigger towing vehicle. Still, I don't feel that my cruising style or access to areas has been compromised.

MULTIHULLS

The very title of this book suggests this category of boats. The kind of beach that comes readily to mind is scarce in Maine, but it isn't hard to imagine a long sandy beach under swaying palm trees, with the brightly colored sails of a multihull fluttering in the late afternoon breeze as it noses gently ashore. Of course I'm probably thinking of a Hobie Cat—a lithe little devil of a speed demon, exhilarating to sail but not well suited to cruising unless you travel in a wet suit with rubber duffel bags tied to the trampoline. Still, the effortless speed, light weight, and beachability of the multihull means it has a lot going for it as a beach cruiser.

I don't discount the Hobie Cat as a suitable cruiser for the adventurous, but there are some designs on the market that offer a drier ride, good storage, and are easily trailerable behind all but the smallest cars. One caveat: with a few exceptions you had better be handy with tools or know a builder since many of the more intriguing designs are available only as homebuilder plans or in kit form.

Catamarans have two hulls, and about the smallest that offers true cruising abilities is the *Tiki*-21—a 600-pound, plywood-and-epoxy boat designed by multihull pioneer James Wharram. This design won the 1982 *Cruising World* magazine competition for new and innovative trailerable boats, being chosen over several monohulls! Each of *Tiki*'s hulls has a single bunk, dry storage, and flotation. For more commodious or connubial accommodation a large tent can be set up on the platform between the hulls (many multihull cruisers carry collapsible lawn chairs and tables). Sailing performance is lively—in the 8- to 12-knot range, much faster than comparably sized monohulls. The *Tiki* has a lot of reserve stability in case of a blow; you won't find yourself hanging over the windward hull to keep her down. Wharram says the *Tiki* can be built in 300 to 400 man-hours, at something like $3,000 in materials—not a bad investment. Like most small multihulls, the boat easily disassembles to the legal trailering width of 8 feet.

A word about multihull sailing. For the most part these boats do not sail upwind as well as monohulls; the reasons should be obvious just by looking at them. A wide beam, not much hull in the water for tracking, and a lot of windage make tacking more adagio than allegro. However, since they are also considerably faster than monohulls, getting there

James Wharram 'TIKI'

might even be quicker, although you cover more ground in the process—
just bear off a bit and crack it on. Another multihull advantages is that
they are great in light air—most can ghost along in next to nothing.

The Wharram designs (from 14 to 70 feet) are well-known for their
simplicity of construction and legendary sea-keeping qualities. Another
designer who has gained a wide reputation for his trimarans (three hulls),
which are perhaps more complex to construct but have few equals for

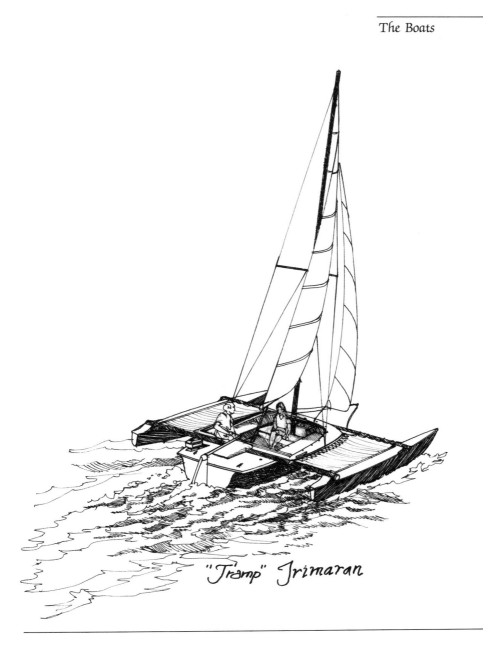

"Tramp" Trimaran

sheer beauty and grace, is Chris White, of South Dartmouth, Massachusetts. The main feature of these boats is the vacuum-molded laminated wood hull panels, which are joined together to make each ultra-strong unit. Chris offers these pre-formed hull panels, called Vari-Cam, as part of a kit for home builders, or you can buy one of his designs ready-made

39

from an authorized boatbuilder. His beachcruiser *Discovery*, is a very practical adaptation of his larger designs, with a secure, dry, 7-foot-square cockpit. The rig is high-tech, with a fully battened mainsail, wing mast, and Harken racing blocks. Performance is impressive, especially for a 20-footer, but comfort is the supreme function of this handsome boat.

Those of you familiar with the reviews in *Small Boat Journal* during the 1980s will remember the thoughtful on-the-water testing of many diverse small craft by my friend Dan Segal and his wife Judy. These reviews would be a good shopping guide for many of the boats in this book, if you have a library nearby with back issues. The majority of the Segal reviews comprise four or six pages in the magazine. But the review of Australian multihull designer Ian Farrier's *Tramp* received nine pages (*Small Boat Journal*, June 1983).

The *Tramp* is a trailerable 19½-foot fiberglass trimaran designed especially for beachcruising. A wide, comfortable cockpit converts to a spacious cabin at night, with a place for everything. Since the whole boat is a stable platform, walking about, sail handling, or just sunbathing on the trampolines doesn't affect the balance. A unique feature is the manner in which the *Tramp* assembles: You don't have to build it at the launching site, just float it off its trailer and swing the outboard hulls up into place. While it is heavier than the catamarans of equal size, aerodynamic hulls and a large, efficient rig give the boat good sailing qualities. (This boat is the direct ancestor of the F-27 from Corsair Marine—a fast, popular cruising trimaran.)

Since almost all multihulls regardless of size draw little water with their centerboards raised, they might be considered beach cruisers en masse, but the larger ones rival the big cruising auxiliaries in price and upkeep, and become rather cumbersome for the weekender to handle. The smaller versions keep it simple and are a good choice, most especially so for families with young children due to their stability and their vast amount of lolling-about space.

Petroleum-powered

POWERBOATS

As evident by the preponderance of information in this book on sailing and its related techniques and gear, it is this author's favorite means of cruising, but I'd be the first to admit that sailing takes more fussing around and preparation than just launching a small motorboat and buzzing off to the nearest good spot, regardless of tide or wind. There are powerboats that are especially inappropriate for beach cruising, but one rather thinks they are also self-exclusionary—their very appearance suggests a different lifestyle and, well, to each his or her own. I have had the pleasure, though, of being acquainted with a few powerboats that are aesthetically pleasing, very able and efficient, or both. In some instances and locations, they may be the only viable means of cruising: rivers with strong currents and generally contrary winds; areas where the distance necessary to reach a suitable site is greater than the ability to sail there in a limited amount of time; and places where there just isn't any reliable wind at all. Not that conditions have to be the sole factor. For some, sailing is not something they adapt to well, or just don't enjoy; others may feel that after years of sailing the activity is a little strenuous, although they are by no means ready for the rocking chair.

Whatever your interests, similar criteria apply in selecting a good powerboat as it does a decent sailing craft: seaworthiness, simplicity, and reliability, and, so that shallows and backwaters can be explored, a manageable draft.

There are many more small outboard boats being manufactured than sailboats; a review of specific models could take up a whole book. Instead, I've chosen to focus on just three that I think embody the essence of the proper beachcruiser.

One thinks of the evolution of transportation as having gone from boat to train to automobile to airplane, but in one instance it turned around and went the other way. After World War II the Grumman Corporation, which had developed sophisticated technology for building lightweight structures from aluminum, found themselves with little market for warplanes. They logically turned to passenger aircraft, but also found a market for boats—most notably canoes and outboard skiffs.

Grumman canoes were and are legendary; many "first editions" are still around—though looking like they'd been in World War II. At the canoeist's pace, the loss of hydrodynamic efficiency due to extreme denting is not critical. The aluminum canoe is still produced, though the newer, "dentproof" space-age materials have become more popular. Fiberglass, Royalex, and Kevlar notwithstanding, the aluminum powerboat takes no back seat to newfangled materials—and is still the boat of choice for many fishermen, clam diggers, and workboat operators.

Dave Getchell, the permanent back page "anchor" of *Boat Journal*, has been traveling the coast of Maine for decades in various "tin skiffs." In his work as developer and director of the Maine Island Trail (see Chapter 4), he has not had the leisure to slowly sail the hundreds of miles he must

41

cover each year to inspect, document, and monitor the many state-owned and private islands on the Trail. This means going about in a wide variety of weather as well, and while you could hardly call his style relaxed, he embodies the very essence of the kind of boating we are trying to define. His gear is simple and compact, his boat well-prepared and well-suited to the local coastal conditions. His current boat is a Lund Alaskan 18 with a 25-h.p. Mariner outboard; although recently acquired, it is a replacement for another Lund he has had for more than 10 years—with probably more than 10,000 sea miles on it. These aluminum skiffs are built in New York Mills, Minnesota—home of the 10,000 lakes and Lord knows how many boats, most of which are outboard powered.

The deep-vee–hulled aluminum "cruiser" is a versatile fishing, beachcruising, and all-purpose workboat. One smaller than 14 feet probably would be vulnerable offshore or in choppy waves, but something around 18 feet seems ideal for most uses. Most of these boats are undecked, and with relatively low freeboard will invite a lot of water on board if going to windward when it's blowing, so gear stowage should be well-thought-out, with waterproof containers. Many can be fitted with spray dodgers, which help keep both gear and crew drier, but some prudent sailing will help as well—quartering through waves instead of punching straight through them for instance.

Though aluminum boats tend to be noisy, they are nearly maintenance-free and will last almost indefinitely. Because they will be beached frequently, they should have several strong skegs on the bottom, and as there is a strong tendency for the hull to flex under stress and pounding, the structure should be well-braced and tied together with seat risers and gussets.

Lund
—Aluminum Outboard

In outboard cruisers, choosing the power is just as important as selecting the boat. You have no doubt seen fairly small runabouts sporting almost overpowering-looking outboards of 100 or more horsepower, but if you have watched them underway it seems that they could offer little more than teeth-rattling speed. At low speeds they plow along nose high; wide open they bounce like mad from wave top to wave top. Aside from the fact that these behemoth powerplants cost as much or more than the boat they are on, their prodigious appetite for gasoline means you will have precious little room left for camp gear by the time you fit the boat out with enough fuel tanks to go anywhere.

The go-fast crowd will have to excuse me if I suggest that you opt for more modest power. On the average open runabout, 25 h.p. is about maximum to balance fuel economy, sufficient power reserves to keep you out of trouble in adverse conditions or tides, and a quiet-running engine at the more graceful speeds suitable to a relaxed journey. Even so, at eight or 10 knots you are going much faster than most sailboats, and can cover quite a lot of cruising territory—if need be, dead to windward.

In the same way in which sail trim and rig is critical to sailboat performance, so is motor trim to the outboard boat. The angle at which the prop lines up with the waterline determines whether the boat is going to plow, that is, push down the bow, making steering hard, or plane, riding fairly level at normal speeds. Each boat is different, but for fuel efficiency as well as safe motoring this balance should be found.

The aluminum runabout looks like, well, a boat. The Boston Whaler doesn't. But it is, and if not likely to warm the heart of a classic watercraft buff, it is a well-designed and unusual boat intended for maximum stability and efficient performance under power. Designed by Ray Hunt, whose string of power and sailboats is as successful as it is innovative, the Whaler's essential design feature is its tri-hull—a moderately deep vee flanked by two shallower vees. The result is a hull that is stable no matter where you are in it, and sure-footed on all points of power. When turning, the grooves formed by the bottom dig in with little sideslip or lean.

The Whaler is steered from a center console, giving the driver maximum visibility and control at all times. While the design keeps the bow high and dry most of the time, it, like the Lund, is an open boat, and a spray hood is a good option for crusiing. Whalers, which are made in sizes from 13 to 21 feet, have a forward storage locker, most have built-in tankage, and all have an unusually large amount of built-in flotation: The company once cut a 13-footer in half and went motoring around in the stern section.

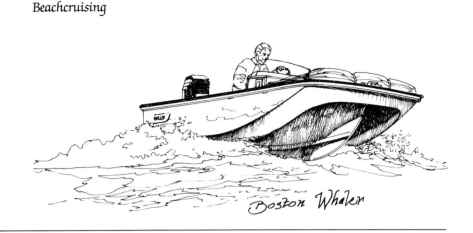

Boston Whaler

There are several clones and spin-offs from this design listed in the sources section of this book; follow the general guidelines for fiberglass boats when looking for a design. The tri-hull adapts well for beachcruising, and with its stability it is especially appealing for families with small children.

Both the aluminum skiff and the fiberglass tri-hull (there are fiberglass mono-hull skiffs available, too) are relatively inexpensive cruisers; generally you can outfit with boat, motor, and trailer for less than $10,000; on the used boat market, considerably less.

While I am promoting the idea that investment in a beachcruiser should be modest so that usable cruising time isn't pre-empted by the need to scramble for the extra income to pay for the cruiser, sometimes a boat comes along that is so elegant and soul satisfying that it's worth the extra investment (we're still talking considerably less than the big marina cruisers). Richard Pulsifer's Hampton boat is such a craft. The term "limited edition" most definitely applies here, thus the reader might question my inclusion of a boat that isn't readily available. In the best of maritime traditions, the Hampton boat is a modern development of one of the best Maine workboats of the 19th century, as well as a finite blend of form, function, and beauty. Since much of the reason we go cruising in the first place is the aesthetic enjoyment of nature, many find the journey much enhanced by such a splendid vessel.

Since the sailing lobsterboats of the last century did not adapt well to power, the Hampton boat, indigenous to Casco Bay on the Maine coast, evolved with a broader stern, flat run, and stiff bilge to make the most efficient use of power. About 20 years ago, Pulsifer took the lines off an existing boat and adapted the construction for strip-building: narrow square strips bent over a form and glued and edge nailed to form a strong hull. The boat is then finished in simple but handsome joinery, though

you could have one built with lots of brass and varnished mahogany if you want. However, I like the fact that it takes its detailing from a workboat heritage; it's also easier to maintain.

For power, Dick uses a 15-h.p. Yanmar diesel — quiet, efficient, and economical. It will push the 22-footer at 12 knots, but having had the opportunity to try a Hampton out I know speed is not as important as its all-around performance. You know you are aboard a thoroughbred; the ride is smooth, rock steady, and the boat moves through a wide variety of conditions with little fuss. I might be stretching it to say that she's a boat that even a diehard sailor would appreciate, but since I am, I do. You can't drag it onto a beach, of course, but you can anchor in water shallow enough to walk ashore. For the right owner, I'd say the Hampton boat would be just the answer.

These powerboats I've been discussing are all open boats, with little real space to sleep aboard conveniently, but there are some cuddy cabin types around — runabouts with small vee-berths forward, mostly under 20 feet. Larger models of this type tend to become pregnant with complicated creature comforts, plumbing, wiring, and other high-maintenance modern inconveniences — and of course they need larger, gas-guzzling engines to drive them.

While this chapter is hardly a comprehensive review of small watercraft, I've tried to show you some of the options available and how they adapt for beachcruising. Clearly there are more choices, but the principle remains the same: simplicity, seaworthiness, and flexibility — at an investment level that gives you the time to get out and enjoy the experience. Since beachcruising is not an exclusive club that requires the right credentials or particular boat to join, it makes no difference whether you go about in a sailboat, powerboat, or rowing craft — just so you go.

45

CHAPTER Two

Gear and Equipment

Lake Huron's Georgian Bay in western Ontario is a wonderful place to go cruising in a small boat. There is a wide variety of islands and inlets to explore and, being just remote enough, it has yet to become too spoiled by commercial development. As a boy I went to a sailing and canoeing camp, on the site of a former Royal Navy training base, called Camp Queen Elizabeth—a name I thought infinitely more suitable than Kamp Wak-Ta-No-Seeum or some other such name taken from an extinct tribe of New Jersey Indians. In all it was a grand place, and probably contributed much to my love of wilderness—the following notwithstanding.

After we had been coached and drilled in canoe handling, our cottage, shepherded by two senior counselors, took off en masse for a three-day, 40-mile adventure. The first day went splendidly until around three in the afternoon, when the wind shifted to the northwest and began to build. Even with three to a canoe we were very tired, very wet young lads by the time we reached our campsite. Not wet enough apparently. Just as we set up our canvas army tents a thunderstorm decided to strike. As I was the last to secure a site, mine was in a slight gully, and having forgotten to dig a trench around it, I passed the night squirming around in a soggy sleeping bag.

After a morning attempt at fire building produced more smoke than fire, I settled for a box of Rice formerly Krispy cereal. As I poured powdered milk into the box, shivering and bedraggled, I watched my counselor—perfectly dry in fresh clothing—walk smugly around checking on his "boys" while enjoying a plate of French toast and bacon and sipping a mug of hot chocolate. I hated him.

This was supposed to be a self-reliance course, a sort of proto-Outward Bound, so our guides weren't really cruel; just supervisors of our self-sufficient attempts to learn to live in the outdoor environment. Later I was one of those counselors myself; no doubt I was just as smug as I watched my miserable troops deal with the same soggy campsite.

Obviously, experience is a great teacher, but without the resilience of youth to keep you going back for more, you may give up before you learn to make it comfortable. While each outing generally provides at least one new circumstance, pleasant or otherwise, preparedness and the preponderance of high-tech gear available today can make even your earliest adventures more palatable.

Keeping Dry

How our servicemen survived the wars in government-issue tents is beyond me. They were heavy, they stank, and if you touched the inside when it was raining—hard to avoid given the cramped quarters—they leaked. Of all the elements that contribute to a beachcruiser's sense of well-being and appreciation of the outdoors, keeping dry—both underway and when you get there—heads the list. Keeping warm (or cool as the case may be) and well-fed are next, but both are directly affected by your state of dryness.

On the water there are many things you can do to ensure this condition. Let's begin with the most vulnerable—the open boat. It will be helpful, of course, if its design keeps out most of the spray. But most open boats have fairly low freeboard. Going to windward, quite a bilgeful of water usually manages to find its way aboard. Accepting that as a given, the objective is to keep both the crew and your gear as dry as possible.

You can start with good foul-weather gear for yourself and waterproof bags for your duffel, but if the day is otherwise warm and sunny, foul-weather gear can be hot and sweaty; you may get just as wet under your foulies as you might have gotten had you left them off. A better alternative is to fit your boat with some sort of spray hood or dodger. It can be simple or complex depending on the layout of your boat, but if it's well-fitted a good dodger is nearly as valuable as a good compass.

Here are several ideas for various types of boat. Some builders offer standard dodgers as an option; in other cases you may have to go to a good canvas shop, or if you are handy, make one yourself. Paul and Mayra Butler's book, *Upgrading Your Small Sailboat for Cruising* (International Marine Publishing, 1988), is an excellent guide to modifying small boats—everything from strengthening hulls and rigs to building-in various clever cruising amenities, including dodgers.

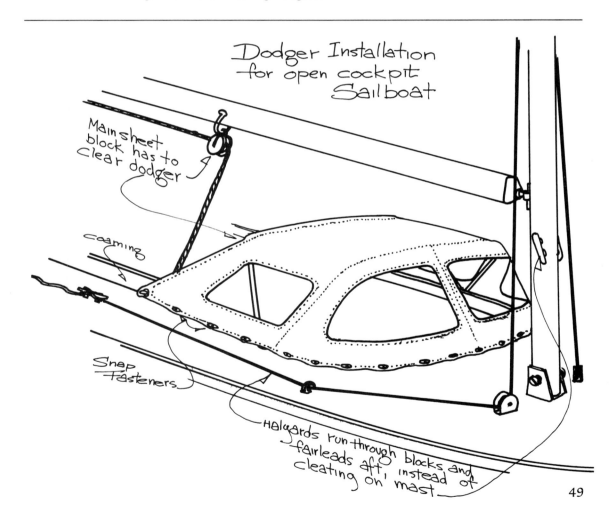

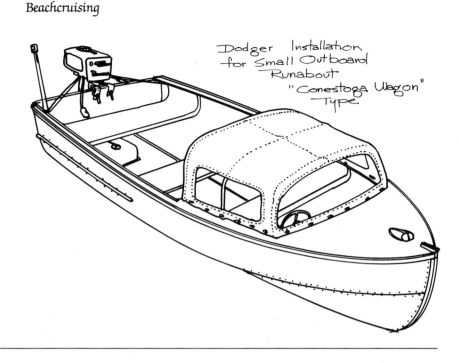

Dodger Installation for Small Outboard Runabout "Conestoga Wagon" Type

The two most important aspects of a good dodger are that it be securely fastened to keep the water out, and that it not interfere with operating the boat—especially since it is likely to be up in adverse conditions, just when you need the most control over your craft.

Even a good dodger will not keep all moisture out of the boat, and rain seems to have a way of insinuating its way forward where you least expect it. Consequently, camping and cruising gear needs to be stored in seriously waterproof duffel bags. At the low end of the scale, plastic garbage bags work in theory—and you ought to have a supply along anyway for a variety of uses. In practice, however, they tear, they leak, and they blow overboard if you turn your back on them for a second. Drawstring sailcloth or canvas bags are stronger but not especially waterproof. The best duffels I've seen and used are the neoprene- or PVC-coated fabric bags with a clever roll-up top that forms a locked handle when fastened. They come in a variety of sizes, and while not dirt-cheap ($10 to $40 depending on size), consider their real value: Properly closed, they and their contents *float*. Think about it.

The larger bags are suitable for clothing, food, and camping gear; the smaller ones can keep cameras, binoculars, and valuables safe and dry. Secured with a small line aboard, they even add flotation to the boat while keeping your gear with you in the odd chance of a capsize. This experience by itself is bad enough, but if you're miles from home without dry, accessible clothing and food, it could be a disaster. I give this simple device four stars; don't leave port without them—even in larger, well-protected boats.

I've been stressing planning. Plan to be wet—especially in an open boat. Even if you have everything carefully packed away in the best of waterproof bags before leaving the dock, unless you have planned carefully you're almost certain to discover that you need something once underway; invariably that something is at the bottom of a large container. Busy with the "running of the ship," after you finally find it you don't put everything back, and before long things find their way into the bilge. Wet things mix with dry things. Soon there *are* no dry things.

Try planning for this at dockside. Instead of thinking of your boat as a kindly, comfortable place, moving gently through a sunny afternoon as you prepare a delightful lunch on board, close your eyes and imagine it heeled over, spray flying, Wrath-of-God rain clouds looming ahead, loose gear sliding all over the place, while you grub around for something—anything—to eat, even soggy saltines. This is an unlikely scenario, but if you plan for it, then some unanticipated disagreeable weather or gusty winds will not spoil your outing.

For yourself and your crew there is so substitute for decent foul-weather gear. Decent, in beachcruising terms, does not have to mean $500 worth of space-age trappings designed for the Whitbread Round the World Race. But on the other end of the spectrum, the type that folds up into a little pouch available for $15 at your local drug store won't serve either.

Boating magazines usually run articles comparing rain gear at least once a year; check out those for basics first, then try some on. At a minimum you'll need a jacket. Here are some basics to look for. Is the fabric waterproof, or just water-resistant? Gore-Tex, for instance, sort of walks the line. It isn't immersion-proof, but it does a good job of shedding water. And unlike totally waterproof fabric, it breathes—an important feature in warm weather, where perspiration collecting inside raingear can soak you. Is it lined, or just a shell? Meaning it might keep you dry, but not warm. Zippers should be of high-quality plastic, not metal, or you might find yourself "rusted in." Pockets and flaps should have Velcro fasteners instead of snaps for the same reason.

If you want to go the whole route, and if your local conditions dictate that you'll encounter wet weather frequently, then a pair of overall-type pants are a good investment. And if you're a really intrepid sailor who isn't stopped by rain, then by all means get a Sou'wester hat, even if people start calling you Captain Ahab. The Black Diamond Company makes a decent, fully rubberized one much favored by commercial fishermen. I can tell you from experience that nothing beats it in really nasty weather.

But it doesn't always rain. When most of us dream of cruising we think warm sunny days. After all, the idea is to pick your weather if you can. But the water is a funny environment. Despite the sun, in all but southern climates, sometimes even there late in the day, the constant wind blowing across cool water—a natural air conditioner and humidifier—makes you damp and gives you a chill. Excellent windbreakers are available tailored for boaters or cyclists, and are highly recommended. The better ones have a flap-back for ventilation; some have a zip-out hood that folds into the collar. One of these over a light sweater will keep you warm on those days when it is chilly but not really cold and wet. Foul weather gear tends to be bulky and will need its own space; windbreakers fold up small and can be tucked into and extricated from a bag easily.

Generally, sea-going clothing should be planned in layers, so items can be added or shed as conditions change. Heavy, bulky clothing would have to be changed altogether. By all means have a full set of dry clothing stowed in one of your waterproof bags.

Keeping Cool

As you might expect, I love sailing in Maine—even though dealing with the weather here often requires a slightly flinty disposition. Lest I appear unsympathetic with the balmy waterways of gentler climes, let me say that we try to sneak out of here in March, which in Maine is 100 days long. Florida beckons to frozen boaters throughout the North, and it is a welcome tonic.

While the sandy beaches, small tides, and virtual absence of rocks and ledges are a delightful change, dealing with the perpetual sunshine can be uncomfortable at times. We all like the image of the well-tanned sailor, but as the protective layer of ozone continues to dissipate in a phritzz of underarm spray and air conditioner effluvia, we of the latter 20th century must guard against skin cancer. Be sensible and moderate in your exposure. Use sunscreens. And to save your eyes from a perpetual squint (or possibly sunburned corneas) invest in a decent pair of polarized sunglasses. If you are like me and do not like the color distortion, at a minimum wear a visor with a long bill.

"Layering" for Foul Weather

Turtleneck Jersey

Light or Medium weight Sweater

Foul-Weather Jacket

Velcro Flaps

Nylon Zipper

If the land of endless summer is where you live, a good means of keeping cool underway or at anchor is to fit a bimini top. Most powerboats make provision for them, but even a small sailboat can be fitted with one. The drawings show some options. You may have to modify your mainsheet so that it is attached to the aft end of your boom (if it isn't there already), and you'll have to make sure your lines clear the bimini's structure on all points of sail.

As important as sun protection is, keeping hydrated is equally so, even in less warm areas. Cool drinks are psychologically refreshing, but even when the ice runs out the important thing is to keep hydrated. Sweet soda, even if taste-tempting, is of little value, but consuming adequate quantities of iced tea, Gatorade, fruit juice, and just plain water is important to avoid heat-exhaustion, headaches, or worse. Sparkling or spring waters come in various flavors, without the added sugar. By all means save the alcohol for the end of the day; it is no thirst quencher, and it impairs your judgment on the water.

Safety Equipment

I don't think you have to sail forth armed to do battle with the North Atlantic in February, but if your cruiser is equipped with some contingency
gear, you will be able to cope with most emergencies without undue
stress.

You can assess your safety needs by examining the environmental
conditions that pose potential hazards. Safety doesn't mean having just a
foghorn, a flare pistol and a first aid kit. Safety means using accumulated
skills and experience to stay out of trouble as well as having the ability to
cope with it. Understanding weather and local conditions will help you to
avoid fighting severe weather or adverse tides; having your boat well prepared for handling in adverse conditions will make it easier to control
when conditions escalate beyond its comfortable sailing ability; and a
little fair-weather practice will make handling emergencies less confusing.
Obviously then, the first item of safety equipment you'll need to acquire is
mental preparedness. Then you'll need the proper gear to implement it.

If you are depending on sail power, you need to be sure your rig is
strong and can be controlled easily. This means being able to reef in
strong winds, possibly even change sails, and all without risking going
overboard. To reduce the area of the mainsail, it must have reef grom-
mets; it should also have reefing lines installed and ready to use to allow
you to reef quickly. Like other emergency procedures, reefing should be
practiced in good weather until you can do it smoothly. An unexpected
line squall is no time to learn reefing.

Essential to the operation is either a topping lift or lazyjacks; otherwise the boom falls into the cockpit when you try to lower sail and you
can't easily work around it. If you have a crew, have someone try to keep
the boat pointed into the wind as you reef; otherwise you have to reach
outboard to do it. If you are singlehanding you could tie the tiller amid-
ships with shock cord while you work, but if you do, do not cleat the
mainsheet: If the boat falls off the wind and is locked down you could
capsize before you get things unscrambled. Don't worry if the bunched
sail below the reef is untidy; you can secure that later. And don't wait
"just a few more minutes" to reef. If you are uncertain, do it. It takes little
time to shake out a reef, but putting one in will seem to take forever if the
wind is slamming you all about. And bear in mind that an uncleated sail,
even in moderate wind, makes a lot of noise. While it is disconcerting, it
is not as dangerous as it sounds. Don't be intimidated by it, just go about
your business.

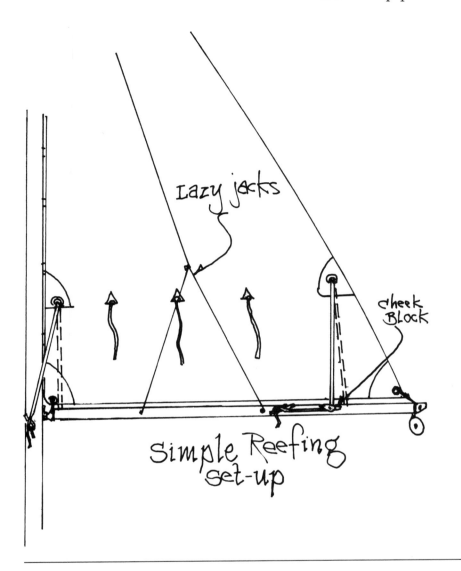

Lazy jacks

cheek Block

Simple Reefing set-up

If you have a jib, the first recourse in high winds is dropping it. The best bit of gear to keep it under control is a bungee cord. You can quickly gather in the sail and take a wrap around it with the cord to keep it from going over the side or travelling back up the forestay.

An even better way to minimize the time you have to spend forward muzzling the jib is to install a roller furling jib, which rolls up like a window shade. Not all furling equipment is created equal, though, and strong winds can sometimes unfurl the sail. Make sure the furling line is secured; if it is a lightweight unit you might want to tie a sail stop around the sail. The better units have an extruded luff groove, which holds the furled sail securely and allows you to sail with it partially unrolled (reefed) to allow you to balance your sailplan for varying conditions. But whatever your boat's rig, being able to control it under all conditions is the first measure of safety.

If you are cruising under power, the best piece of safety equipment is a well-maintained engine, along with ample reserves of fuel. It also helps to be familiar with the basics of maintenance and troubleshooting, and have along the appropriate spares and tools for minor repairs. If the boat is small enough, have along one or two sets of oars as a back-up. In larger boats, do as many experienced powerboaters do: mount a small two- or four-horse outboard to one side on the transom. It'll pay for itself in emergencies, or by sparing your main outboard the onerous task of trolling (constant slow-speed running fouls spark plugs).

No proper boat should be without a compact but adequate tool and repair kit. A small fishing tackle box filled with the common tools will work fine. Be sure you have a pair of Vise-Grips—one of the most indispensable fix-it tools. Bring along a roll of duct tape—more major disasters have been avoided temporarily with this stuff than anything I can think of. You'll need spare rig or engine parts (spark plugs, shear pins, fuel filter, cotter keys, shackles, cable clamps, etc.). Sturdy twine and wire, a small folding saw, a sailor's knife or, if you prefer, a good Swiss Army knife—though not one with 62 blades. It's an interesting novelty, but all those little doodads are hard to actually use.

The Coast Guard has a set of mandatory minimums for safety equipment for various classes of boats; you'll want to check for the gear specified for your boat. Just having safety gear aboard isn't enough, however; stow the items where they are easily accessible.

For your peace of mind, if you are the skipper, establish a rule that non-swimmers aboard should be wearing, not sitting on, a life jacket. In rough conditions weak swimmers must (and sensibly, everybody should) be wearing one. I can hear the protest now: "they're too hot, too bulky, it's such a nice day, nothing could happen."

I'll be the first to admit that forcing your crew to wear life jackets is not easy, unless you aspire toward a reputation as a nouveau Captain Bligh. Some discretion often is necessary. It might help to illustrate the wisdom of it all if you stage a make-believe man overboard situation (a good idea anyway). Throw an apple or an orange overboard, ask one of your crew to pretend it is you—the captain and presumably the person on

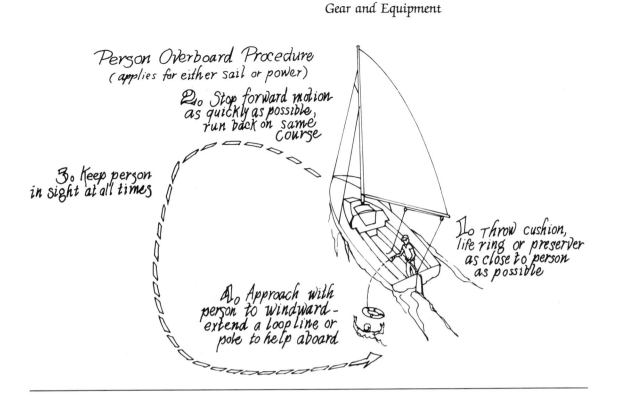

Person Overboard Procedure
(applies for either sail or power)

2. Stop forward motion as quickly as possible, run back on same course

3. Keep person in sight at all times

1. Throw cushion, life ring or preserver as close to person as possible

4. Approach with person to windward — extend a loop line or pole to help aboard

board most skilled at handling the boat — and have them try to retrieve it. If they're complete novices, first walk them through the exercise yourself. Keep track of the time it takes, bearing in mind that hypothermia is a factor if a person has to spend more than a few minutes under stress in deep water. This is especially important in northern waters; even in the middle of August the Atlantic waters north of Cape Cod rarely pass 50 degrees.

This is a sobering argument in favor of life preservers. Having said that, I should mention that not all life preservers have to look as though you're abandoning ship after being torpedoed on the Murmansk run. There are many lightweight vests available — some developed for waterskiers, canoeists, and sailboarders. Small "fanny packs" are available that self-inflate upon entry into the water, and some manufacturers, notably Sterns, produce "float-coats" — normal-looking windbreakers or foul-weather gear with built-in flotation (although this is likely to be too warm for hot-weather use).

Electronic Dependency

Hand-held or bulkhead-mounted VHF radios could be considered safety equipment; certainly they have the virtue of providing around-the-clock, up-to-date weather information, and they enable you to contact the Coast Guard in an emergency. They are fairly expensive, however, ranging from $125 to $500 or more, and while they have played an important part in many rescue operations, you should not regard them as providing ultimate security. It takes time for a Coast Guard vessel or helicopter to reach you, and few small boat operators are skilled enough to give exact positions. Even three square miles of moderately rough ocean is a vast territory when looking for a 20-foot boat.

And VHF has a tendency to breed complacency; after all, help is just a call away. Often calls are made when the situation, although unpleasant, is not really life threatening. Think carefully before calling. There are limited rescue craft in a given area; the inconvenience "distress" call may be depriving someone else in a real emergency. Also you should be aware that the Coast Guard now charges for towing, or turns you over to a commercial tow on site; this can be very expensive. The use of a radio is your right and free choice, but don't use it to take the place of self preparedness.

If you are sailing in foggy areas, a radar reflector will help larger vessels, most of which are equipped with radar, locate you. This reflective device folds up small, but can be hoisted aloft to make your blip more visible on a radar screen. Still, it is your duty to be alert. Even if they see you in time, most ships and commercial vessels can't maneuver in time to avoid collisions with small craft. It is your duty to stay out of their way.

As for mounting radar on a beachcruising–size boat? No doubt some day they will be miniaturized to the size of a Walkman and sell for very little more, but for now even the smallest radars are too bulky for the kinds of boats we're talking about, and cost about as much as your trailer, a new engine, or a set of sails. If you are practicing the art of beachcruising, you'll soon get the hang of fog, and probably enjoy re-telling your adventures as you successfully and safely run a passage home in a real pea-souper.

There are some low-tech hints that are useful in fog. Though our ears are no match for the dolphin's sonar, if you sit quietly, with the radio off, you might pick up shore sounds, and by their intensity, determine how far offshore you are. You might call this dog-bark navigation. Going slow is the best plan—you can generally "hear" a shoaling ledge before you can see it. Scan up and down as well as from side to side—some fog banks are quite low, and often the tops of trees on islands will show through the thinner gray.

ANCHORING

For obvious reasons, also included under safety is the art of anchoring. There may be occasions when emergency anchoring is your only option—drifting down on rocks in a foul tide with your mast and outboard broken, for a grim but unlikely example. But for the most part, safety when anchoring means you want to be able to drift off to sleep while anchored with the knowledge that you will stay where you are.

Select an anchor matched to your boat. The Danforth company labels its with a range—that is, "will hold 15- to 20-foot boat in winds up to 25 knots." That doesn't take into account all factors, but it is a guide. I like an anchor one size up from the recommendation for an extra margin of safety. For small boats, the Danforth type, shown here, is about the best all around design. You will need to add some anchor chain to hold down the stock and prevent it from lifting free, and you'll need an anchor rode. For small boats you will want at least 75 to 100 feet of good nylon rode; probably ³/8-inch diameter is best (smaller line will hold most

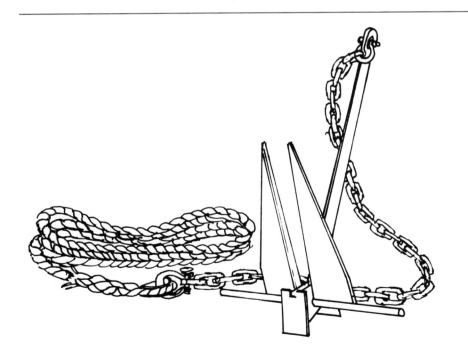

beachcruisers, but it's hard to grip). A smaller "lunch hook" with 30 feet or so of line is good for a backup, and for short stops in calm conditions.

Whole books have been devoted to the art and science of anchoring, but for most beachcruising, two or three basics will do. Determine where to anchor by using the best information you can get about the holding ground, available either from the markings on the charts, from cruising guides, or local advice from experienced boaters. Mud, sand, and loose rock are the best holding grounds; shale, ledge, and thick kelp beds the poorest. Naturally the best shelter is away from the prevailing breeze, but often good anchorages can be found in shallower bights that are somewhat more exposed, especially if there is a high tree or rock line above it.

As you reach your spot, lower your anchor steadily until you sense it hitting bottom. Don't throw it; it may foul on the way down and prevent the flukes from digging in. Now let out enough scope—about five times as much rode as the water is deep at high tide—to keep the anchor stock horizontal and act as a shock absorber. Be sure to leave enough swinging room—if you anchor at high tide, your circle will be greater at low tide.

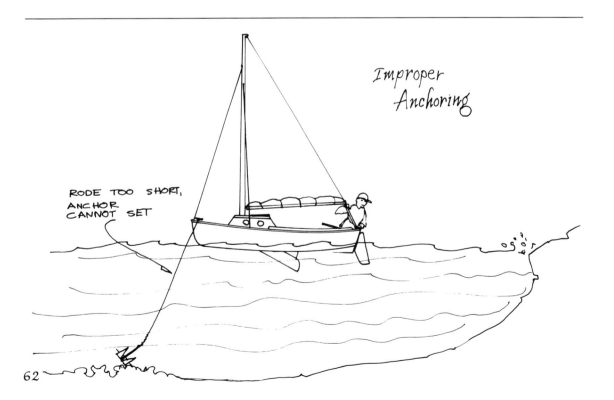

Improper Anchoring

RODE TOO SHORT, ANCHOR CANNOT SET

Check the chart for depth at mean low water to estimate. Secure your rode to the bow cleat, and if you expect heavy weather, wrap a plastic guard or a piece of hose around the line where it passes over the rail to prevent chafe. To up-anchor, reverse the process. Haul yourself up to the anchor until you're right over it, with the rode vertical.

Anchoring applies to boats that are beached as well. In tidal areas, unless you are very familiar with your local beaches and the range of tide, you might find yourself adrift when you least expect it. Also, if you are "bow beaching," a stern anchor will keep the rest of your boat from swinging around and getting stuck. You can use it to pull your boat backwards off the beach, like navy landing craft.

Camping, Cooking, and Gear

I've alluded to the advantages beachcruisers have gained from the proliferation of high-tech backpacking gear. When you think that hikers have to carry all the equipment and provisions they'll need on their backs, just imagine the creature comforts you can stow in even a small daysailer.

A good tent is the first option for the open-boat owner to consider. With one, even the smallest open boat can have rather sumptuous accommodations. But even if you have a small cabin on your cruiser, a modern tent stows away in such a small space that having one aboard gives you the option of camping ashore whenever you like. And if you are cruising with kids it might be a great peacemaker.

Dome tents are the best choice for beachcruising. They are largely self supporting, and thus can be set up on a sandy beach or other location not suitable for tent stakes. Tents come in all grades and prices. Base your selection on the amount of use you expect to give it. But with tents, as

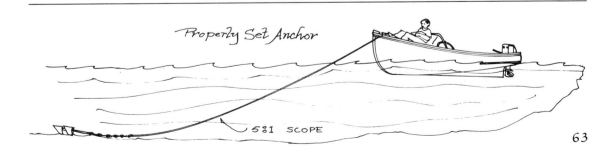

Properly Set Anchor

5∶1 SCOPE

with most everything else, you get what you pay for. In the long run, top-quality gear is still the best investment—especially since as a beachcruiser you aren't paying marina fees, yard bills, and buying $67 stainless steel snap-shackles every week.

Ashore, or in your boat, it's time to take your comfort seriously. Watching old westerns, I've always wondered what sort of a night's sleep a cowboy had on hard ground with nothing more than a blanket roll, and maybe his saddle for a pillow. I don't even want to think about his grub—biscuits made from bug-infested flour and fried prairie dog maybe—we've come a long way, at least in wilderness camping.

I'll get to sleeping bags in a moment, but let's start from the ground up. Bags are for thermal comfort but offer little padding. There are two basic types of ground pad—roll-up foam or self-inflating air. The latter rolls tight, and you just have to open the valves—the pad absorbs the air it needs. The degree of comfort varies with the thickness and design—it's best to examine your choice in person rather than rely on mail order. For the ultimate, an air mattress is closest to your bed at home, but it is bulkier to carry, and requires either a pump or a healthy set of lungs to inflate. In keeping with the old adage that you get what you pay for, buying an air mattress in a chain department store is to take the chance that by morning your hip will be resting on a rock.

Given that outdoor adventurers on land and sea are likely to go exploring in a wide range of environments, it is understandable that there would be different sleeping bags available to suit each need. this seems to be an area of overkill for some reason. One catalog I received has 13 pages of just sleeping bags alone. For marine purposes the criteria is somewhat simplified: temperature, size, and water resistance. In the better outfitters' catalogs such as L.L. Bean, Cabela's, and REI, bags are rated for thermal comfort, that is, the lowest temperature at which the bag can maintain normal body heat. Most beachcruising is a three-season activity, but you will have to determine which bag *generally* suits your

65

overall temperature range. Size categories are the mummy bag—small in stowage but rather confined in warm temperatures; the full-zipper rectangular, or the zip-together double for "couple comfort." Most important to beachcruisers is water resistance. Most of the better bags have water-resistant covers, but the filling is what makes the ultimate difference. The goose down so favored by hikers because it packs down small and fluffs up high and provides warmth, has a drawback in the marine environment—if it gets wet it stays wet. DuPont Quallofil maintains 85 percent of its insulation value even when wet, and dries out more rapidly than down or kapok fillings.

For light adequate enough to read that book you've been saving for the trip, there are some excellent choices. The traditional Coleman lantern is still preferred by some—it does give a very bright light, but it is bulky, and you have to carry a flammable fuel for it. Modern batteries are more effective and longer lasting than they used to be, and some are rechargeable. Light sources vary from fluorescent to quartz, and there are even some portable bug zappers on the market.

You can add a number of personal choice items to the comfort list, depending on your preferences and carrying capacity. A bug net tent that drapes over the entire cockpit might be nice if you frequent mosquito- or black-fly infested areas—especially during their feeding time—your morning or evening meal. There are ground-level, folding, back-support type chairs that don't take up much space and make unwinding after a strenuous day of sailing just a little nicer.

The appendix lists a variety of outfitting companies—few manufacturers will sell factory direct and your best bet is to visit a good outdoor store in your area to inquire about the products listed. Though not a requirement, most outdoor store employees are usually camping, hiking or sailing buffs themselves and are happy to share experiences—along with their sales pitches.

Pest Patrol

While we're on the subject of being comfortable in the outdoors, we need to talk about the one thing that stands almost universally between outdoorspeople and comfort: bugs. I have a tried and true method of dealing with Maine's legendary black fly and mosquito squadrons that arrive every year in May. I don't go cruising until June. Or at least if I do I seek an offshore island with a steady breeze blowing over it.

The plain facts: There is very little you can do about bugs, although the little that you can do may keep you a bit more comfortable—at least part of the time. Generally, if you're moving you are fine, but in the early morning or evening, just when you are relaxing at anchor or lolling around the beach, bugs are at their hungriest. If you have to be outside, a strong, woodsman's-type bug dope is probably your best bet, along with exposing as little prime flesh as possible. DEET is the effective ingredient in this stuff, but there is evidence that it can be harmful over time, particularly for children (not to mention it melts any plastic object—eyeglasses for instance—it comes in contact with). Some cruisers swear by Avon's Skin-So-Soft, which seems to repel most pests, at the cost of smelling like a D.A.R. silver tea. Citronella candles and oils are effective in moderate conditions. If you are ashore, your tent's mosquito netting provides the best refuge, but afloat, it's often a choice between suffocating in a closed-up cabin or letting the critters in through the vents.

If your boat doesn't come with screens, either make some or buy them—even for the small vents. If you live in a bug-infested area like Maine or Florida Bay, but still want to sit out in the cockpit in the evening, you might rig up a mosquito net over the cockpit, like those that cover beds in 1940s movies about the tropics. Bulk mosquito netting is available from many camping outfitters.

If, despite your best efforts, you wind up as the main course, don't ruin the rest of your cruise by scratching the leftovers until you become infected. Use a good antiseptic lotion or astringent. And while on the subject, a good first aid kit should be a permanent fixture on your boat, even for day trips. Carry the usual assortment of bandages, antiseptics, sterile pads, lotions, sunblocks, and aspirin or non-aspirin pain relievers. To this I would add a bottle of pure aloe vera—a natural product with wonderful healing properties, completely non-toxic, that is good for cuts, bruises, bites, and sunburn.

The Galley

If you wander around the camping department of a good outdoor outfitter like L.L. Bean, you will see an incredible array of stoves, cooking utensils, and gadgets for preparing meals on the trail. There are stoves for every use, from weekending to high-altitude expeditions, fueled by almost everything: propane, white gas, kerosene, butane, alcohol, Sterno, and even solar power. Marine supply stores offer the standard two-burner alcohol or propane stoves common to most small cruisers, as well as single-burner sterno or bottled-propane stoves with gimbaled bulkhead mounts so they stay level when cooking underway.

The choice is yours, but here are some points to consider: If you are a "full meal" cooker, you won't be very happy with a small, single-burner, white-gas stove designed to heat enough water for a solo climber's freeze-dried dinner. If you are going to cook on board or in a cabin, you'll need as safe a stove as possible, either bottled butane, or a low-pressure Coleman. Sterno stoves are compact and safe but you'll be hard put to boil more than a pint of water on one. And don't even think of pancakes—unless you like them runny. Still, they work well as an auxiliary to keep the coffee, soup, or stew warm. I use one to back up my own choice for a stove: a Peak 1 Coleman single burner, which burns white gas (a multi-fuel version, which burns kerosene or white gas, is available as well). The Peak 1 gives good, steady heat, is relatively easy to operate, and is small enough to fit in my galley box.

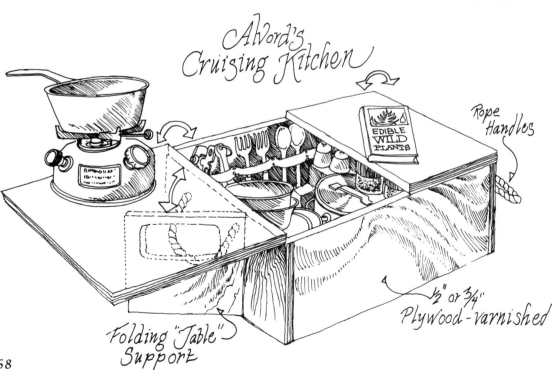

Alvord's Cruising Kitchen

Rope Handles

EDIBLE WILD PLANTS

Folding "Table" Support

½" or ¾" Plywood - varnished

In a given year I am likely to go cruising in my canoe, an open day-sailer, our cuddy cabin sloop, or our vintage Saab 99. Since it seems silly to have different gear for each, I've devised the galley box pictured here. Everything I need, from stoves to silver, is in the box. And it, along with a crate of foodstuffs, is kept at the ready. Should the weather promise a fair wind, or a far-away country fair lure us inland, it's an easy decision to go. The size is up to you—what you have to lug and how many you have to feed. Mine was determined by an existing well in the forward end of *White Heron*'s cabin. With rope handles it hauls out to the cockpit with ease, and since everything fits in it, I have no pots, silverware, and plastic cups rattling around in the bilge or on the bunks.

OUTFITTING THE GALLEY FOR CRUISING

Unless you plan to tow a trash barrel, I'd suggest avoiding the paper-and-plastic—picnic section of your supermarket. Along with the presumption that you are a responsible cruiser and will leave no trash on the beach or chuck your garbage in the ocean, the best argument for not using plastic utensils and paper plates is that they are both ineffective and, for the sailing gourmet, quite unacceptable in style. If you must, use the molded, thicker plates and bowls, but consider that it's going to wind up in somebody's landfill somewhere.

A good alternative is some inexpensive flatware, a few Melmac-type plates, and some deep, sturdy plastic bowls; look for ones with very flat bottoms. You have to wash them of course, but since you aren't going to flop down in front of the tube after dinner anyway, it will take just a few minutes. You can boil up a little dishwater if you want, but cold will work as well, either salt or fresh, though you might want to do the final rinse in a little fresh water. Joy dish detergent is traditional and will rinse free with saltwater, but you might want to consider non-phosphate based soaps, since they don't pollute if disposed of overboard or on the shore.

I use a scrub cloth such as Golden Fleece for the sticky stuff. The trick is to pour some water in the pots while you are eating, and don't let the eggs or chili residue dry on till morning.

For cookware, the ubiquitous aluminum Boy Scout cook kit will work for solo cooking, but it's a little too small and light for anything more substantial. Stainless steel nesting cookware is readily available; it cleans easier than aluminum, retains heat better, and will last forever. Some sets have folding handles, which helps with the stowing, but check them out to make sure they are substantial.

Despite its weight, for years I've carried a good black iron skillet. There is nothing better for pancakes or uniform heat when you need it.

With a pot inverted over it I've managed some pretty decent biscuits, too. Keep it in a separate plastic bag to minimize rusting.

Some small items well worth including: matches in waterproof containers, mitt-type pot holders, various plastic containers with snap-on lids for mixing and storage.

Since you have gone to all the trouble to find the perfect anchorage and are preparing an elegant evening meal on the rocks, why not have tucked away in your supplies a couple of candles, some attractive napkins, and a small picnic-size tablecloth—even some plastic wine glasses, which look elegant even if they aren't crystal. A few wildflowers for the table, perhaps some music on the radio or cassette player, and even the simpler fare becomes more enjoyable. The fanciest restaurant on earth would have a hard time matching the decor provided free by nature.

Depending on the food you bring (see Chapter 5), you probably don't need an ice chest the size of a foot locker. For really carefree, spur-of-the-moment cruising, you may learn to get along without one at all, or at best with a small cooler for frozen items. The space you have inboard will pretty much determine the size of your cooler anyway. One idea is to have two small ones—one for the main course items, fresh or frozen, and one for beverages. The first can be left closed until needed, the other will be opened more frequently. Some types have a built-in ice bottle under the lid, but they are not very effective in really hot weather. While some like the convenience of "blue ice" (gelled refrigerant sealed in plastic), I prefer to freeze water or juice in paper or plastic milk container. I can use it as it thaws, so it does double duty.

A good thermos is a boon. It's nice to have hot soup or a beverage available throughout the day on a cool fall cruise without firing up the stove. The stainless steel types are especially efficient, although expensive. But because they will outlast dozens of the fragile glass type, they're worth the money.

To aid cooling, an idea borrowed from the old pioneer canteen works well. Either make or buy ready-made heavy canvas covers for the thermos bottle. Wet down the whole thing in the morning and the evaporation will keep the contents cool. For hot lunches underway, small, individual wide-mouth plastic thermos jars are good for soup, stew, or the like. These can be prepared in the morning and wrapped in a towel for extra insulation.

There is no delicate way to bring up the subject of waste disposal, but in a society that hopefully is edging toward responsible waste management, the old cedar bucket, simple as it might have been, is no longer an ecologically sound idea. It may be impractical on a small daysailer, but if you can accommodate one, a portable toilet is the most responsible means of waste disposal. Most types have an easily removable tank that can be dumped into a convenient toilet at home or in a filling station. This may be inconvenient, but it's better than overboard discharge. If you keep the chemical deodorizer fresh, there should be no unpleasant odors, though in most small cruisers it's a good idea to keep the Porta-Potti in the cockpit at night—probably a better place to use it, too. If you are camping on an island, take it ashore if you can. If you must use "nature's outhouse," dig a deep hole, and after you're done refill it carefully. A good idea, too, is to use biodegradable toilet paper available from marine supply or camping stores. The brands formulated for marine sanitation dissolve in water.

Now that you have all this stuff, go back to the basics of beachcruising—planning and preparedness. Decide where you'll keep things so they are accessible, and if necessary, dry. Experience will tell you which things you can do without and which are indispensable so that you wind up with familiar gear that is neither too little nor too much.

Though you might not consider this last item as gear, a small supply of field guides to wildlife, flora and fauna, geology, or marine history may extend your cruising pleasure. If you just want to lie back and watch it all go by, washing away the clutter of life ashore may be accomplishment enough, but after a while you may find you are relaxed enough to broaden your interests into how the rest of life on this planet functions.

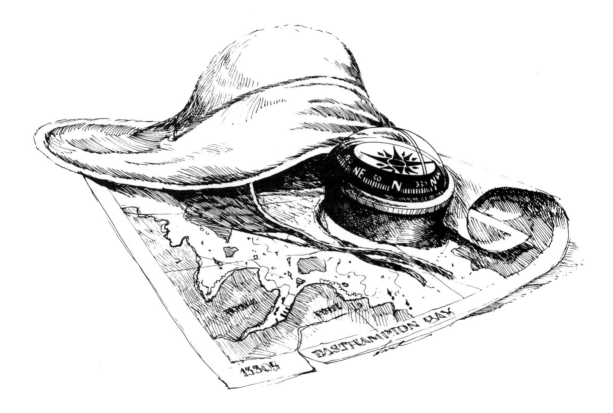

CHAPTER Three

Getting There: Navigation and Weather

As a small-boat sailor, I've often felt the frustration of trying to work to windward on one of those hot July afternoons when the sea is glassy and the breeze, if you could call if that, comes and goes at will. You don't seem to be making progress, and to make matters worse, a graceful 50-footer slowly passes you by, her tall sails full and drawing. You scratch your head and say, "How is that possible? I'm so light I should move in a whisper and that thing must weigh tons." It does, and so does a freight train, and that, in part, explains why it can make speed in light air. In a word, momentum: Its greater weight, once in motion, will carry farther under the same conditions than a lighter boat.

The other factor working in the large boat's favor is that its heavy displacement and deep keel will support a very large sail plan. In theory, if you could put a proportionally large rig on a dinghy it would do pretty well, too, until the first strong gust capsized it. Yet well before the leisure class took to the water, fishermen went about in small boats regularly and in all kinds of weather. The secret to their sailing ability was less in their boats and more in their intimate knowledge of their local sailing grounds, including tides, normal weather patterns, and seasonal changes.

For example, fishermen usually got underway very early in the morning, often rowing to a fishing spot upwind. It isn't that they were early risers by nature. It's just that in summer the dawn hours are traditionally calm and, since they haven't hauled traps or lines all day, they're fresh for rowing and their boat is light and unburdened. After an exhausting day's fishing and, hopefully, a full boat, they'd ride the onshore breeze home in the afternoon with a small sprit or lateen rig. Of course if it didn't work out that way they had another trick: patience. If the wind was contrary they would just make long tacks, trying to make the most out of the shore breeze—and get home when they could.

Since I've noticed little change in either the wind or the ability of small boats to beat it, something of the fisherman's techniques will still benefit us fair-weather sailors. True, modern boats and rigs are more sophisticated and efficient, but at three or four knots we're not talking about much of an advantage. And even though a powerboat is not as dependent on wind and tide, taking advantage of favorable winds and currents makes for better fuel economy and is easier on the boat and engine.

Assuming that most of your beachcruising will be done close to home, begin to familiarize yourself with local weather and wind patterns for each season. For instance, where I live in mid-coast Maine the prevailing summer breeze is southwest, although close to land it tends to start northwest in the early morning. On a typical summer day it also seems to take a lunch break, going nearly flat at noon as it clocks slowly around, builds, and by tea time it's blowing pretty well. Evenings tend to be quiet in summer, so you want to be where you want to be by then or you'll have to row or motor. (Which is okay too—this isn't hairshirt voyaging, remember.)

Setting aside chart navigation for the moment, let's assume your destination is an island—let's call it Green Island and, just for the heck of it, put it in Maine's Penobscot Bay—about three or four miles offshore and five miles to the north of the launching ramp. You can see it, perhaps you've lived within sight of it for a while, and you don't really need a chart to get there. But if it's to be a successful and enjoyable trip, you will need to know such things as how the currents set, and where any underwater hazards might be, for instance. Ask the local boaters.

Time and tide, as they say, wait for no man, but both can be used to advantage by smart skippers of either gender. One solution to getting to Green Island would be to launch north of it in the morning, ride the offshore breeze down for lunch, and ride the afternoon southwesterly back to your trailer. But that's too easy and, besides, there's probably no launching ramp there anyway.

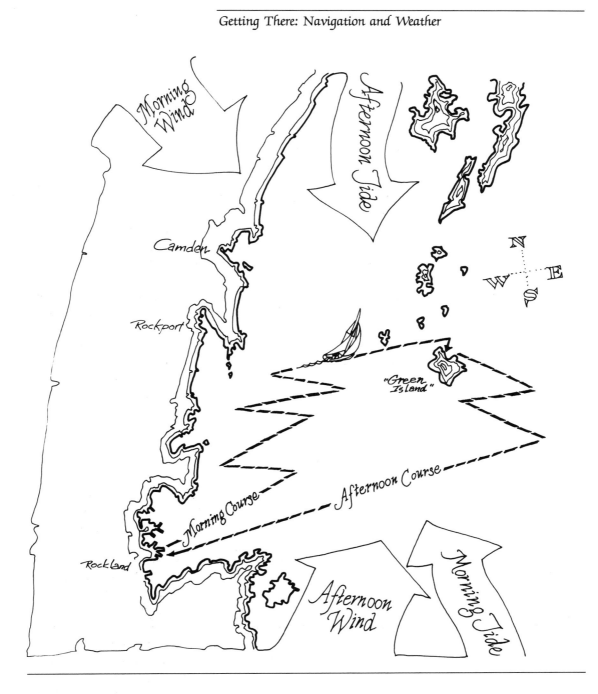

A look at the tide chart tells you low water will be at 6 a.m. This is good, since Penobscot Bay has a northerly flow on the flood tide, and high tide will be about noon. However, the morning wind is northwest, so you can't sail directly up the bay. You take a tack out, say half a mile, and then work back toward the land where the wind will be strongest. The tide will be helping, giving you at least an extra knot. In good fashion you should reach the island by high water on a dozen or so tacks. For now let's say this is a day trip, so after a fine lunch and a stroll around (you might just pick up a little trash that some other, less considerate, visitor has left behind), it's time to go home. But now the wind has gone southwest—against you again. So it's not going to be perfect. What is? But you do have the tide with you again and, though the wind is fresher, by making one or two long tacks offshore you can come home on a reach after a spirited sail.

Fine, you say, but what if the tide is wrong, the "local" conditions have taken the day off, and to boot, it looks like rain. Here's the key: Either don't go at all or go someplace else. If you like advanced chess, take the challenge and map out a strategy of your own. If the tide is against you, you could sail out across it until it begins to slacken, then work northerly, or you could make short tacks closer to shore where the current, on coastal areas, tends to be slower. What we are talking about here is 10 minutes of planning based on local knowledge and your best estimate of the day's conditions—and the ability to resist the temptation to sail downwind in the morning when you know there's a better than even chance you will have to tack homeward against a dying breeze in the evening.

Naturally, if this is to be a two- or three-day cruise, you have more latitude in planning and can "waste" a favorable tide to take advantage of a good breeze. And if you are sailing in a lake, of course, you won't have tides to worry about. These techniques apply to rowing and motoring as well, for the action of a prevailing wind and sea on any light-displacement boat is significant. As any runabout skipper can tell you, going to windward in a chop can make for a very wet and dicey ride. To a greater or lesser degree, all small boats need to work with sea conditions.

If in the end it does not work out despite your planning, and Green Island stays just maddeningly out of reach, be prepared to alter course— you just might find something equally as interesting elsewhere.

For those of you primarily interested in motor cruising, it may seem that we go on ad nauseam about the fine points of making that extra half-mile in a four-knot sailboat. But bear with us—some of these strategies apply to efficient powerboating, too.

There are some techniques in sailing that will help make the most of your course made good. Begin with the premise that most small boats just do not sail to windward very well. There are exceptions to every rule, and the exceptions here are racing dinghies, but these boats require acrobatics, clenched teeth, and a wetsuit—hardly laid-back beachcruising.

The cardinal rule when going to windward is do not "pinch," or try to sail too closely upwind. A 500-pound boat can be virtually stopped by a small wave if hit head on in moderate to light air. And if the breeze is strong enough to power the boat through the wave, the ride will be very wet. Rather than pinching in tight, take moderately high tacks. If the wind is gusty, play the mainsheet—close hauling as long as you can until the heeling becomes uncomfortable, then easing off in the puffs.

Generally, too, on an easier tack angle, the boat stays more upright, the way a sailboat was meant to be sailed—despite the glossy photos in racing magazines—and thus tends to move faster. You may sail a greater distance, but the speed made good will nearly offset the lack of forward angle. You are more likely to have a better and drier ride with a pleasant rhythm, too, instead of the bone-jarring crash of wave bucking.

Unless the wind is very steady and not too strong, never tie off the mainsheet unless you have a jam cleat. Even then the sheet should be ready to hand so you can release it easily. It's very tempting to slump down in the boat and gaze up at the clouds, drink in hand, but if you are not alert or prepared, you may be the one in the drink.

So much for windward work. If small boats don't do as well in that category, surely they must just fly downwind. After all, they don't weigh anything, and with all that wind behind them. . . . Not exactly. Don't forget the freight train. The big boats have all that weight and a deep keel to keep them steady. In heavy air, the mainsail can overpower a small boat. It may tend to bury its bow, especially if the waterline is short, or it may swing about as the air pressure tries to make it go faster than it can. Save in light air, the best strategy is to run off at a slight angle from the wind instead of directly before it. This will help avoid a breech or a jibe— the boom coming suddenly over just when you don't expect it. When you have gone as far as you can on one tack you can jibe by gradually hauling in on the sheet as you slowly bring the stern through the wind, then releasing the sheet smoothly as the boom goes over. This will avoid the sudden lurch, save heads, gear, and in heavy air, the very real possibility of a capsize.

If it is to be a long downwind leg and you have a jib, you can help balance the boat by using a whisker pole, or even a boathook, to wing out the jib on the opposite side from the mainsail. As for spinnakers: I like to look at their colorful display, but I don't like to use them, especially since I tend to sail alone or shorthanded. There are those who do like them, but they are probably more adept in their use than I. If you are among them, well, you add to my scenery on a sunny day. There is a nice cruising alternative, though: the light air drifter. This is made of light cloth and shaped somewhere between a spinnaker and a fully cut jib. Its advantage is that it is set completely on one side like a jib, using a pole to hold it out—and can generally be handled by one person.

Minus the rig, rowboats and powerboats can take advantage of the same course of direction—using the wave action to work for rather than against you. In powering, adjust engine speed to crest the waves at a rhythm that does not find you punching through every other wave. Downwind, a following sea can make your craft slew around if your boat speed is not compatible with it.

When rowing, it is essential to "go with the flow" in a seaway, saving your arms and avoiding an unstable motion for the boat. Obviously, trying to row against a heavy tide run is folly unless you are a Goliath. But quartering off across it can keep you making forward motion if you can't wait it out. All three forms of boating are nearly the same if you consider their "rigs" as simply their forms of propulsion. The water and wind will act nearly the same on them all.

Navigation

What I've described so far is "seat of the pants" navigation and boat handling. It really is the basis for the majority of short cruises in nearby waters. This is not meant to replace charted or dead reckoning techniques—all are valuable, worth learning and, on longer trips or under adverse conditions, essential. While I don't intend to write a primer on the more sophisticated aspects of navigation, learning the rudiments of chart reading and basic piloting practices can extend your enjoyment of beachcruising by making it safer and more efficient. For those who want to study the subject in depth, there are several good books available— among them, *The Practical Pilot,* by Leonard Eyges (International Marine, 1989). Its subtitle, "Coastal navigation by eye, intuition, and common sense," is what beachcruising implies. It is a very clearly written text with good illustrations, and while some of the techniques are fairly technical, each is coupled with a down-to-earth example and gives even the amateur a good understanding of the principles of small-boat navigation.

If we are espousing a carefree, pack-it-and-go attitude about cruising, then why delve into the more finite matters of course plotting and chart reading? The answer lies distinctly in the eternal nature of the sea or any other waterway: The sea doesn't take into account that you are only out for the afternoon or an overnight or that your boat is too small for the approaching storm. Nor does the wind feel the need to alter direction to avoid blowing you into some rocky ledge. Going about in boats *safely* is not always easy, but without some basic sea knowledge and a few skills, a warm summer day that begins with sparkling blue skies and gentle winds can end tragically.

The sad fact is that most recreational boating accidents happen close to shore and are caused largely by inexperience or inadequate equipment. I'll discuss how to maneuver safely in more detail in the section on weather, but I emphasize it here since accurate navigation is an important aspect of safe boating.

Navigating can also be entertaining and—when you have laid a course, adjusted somewhere along the way for a shift in conditions, and then smiled as you step ashore just where and when you expected—satisfying. It might not rank with hitting Nuku Hiva right on the nose after 3,000 miles of open-water voyaging, but I'm always rather pleased with myself when I manage to hit a planned destination just about when I expected, and over the course line I intended. It's another of the quieter values of this kind of boating: At a time when our choices of where to go are limited by overcrowding, and the routes to getting there are restricted, channeled, and unimaginative, a little self-reliance and self-testing against modest conditions is a good measure of self-worth.

To navigate you need only a few simple tools. Nautical charts for your area and a good compass are the two essentials; a set of parallel rules and a divider will help; and a decent pair of binoculars will assist in reading land or navigation marks.

READING A NAUTICAL CHART

This is the part you can start in your living room. If you are going to rely on aids to navigation to set your course it's a good idea to become very familiar with the terms and types now. Going about on the water is very different from land travel—nothing looks even remotely the same, even when sailing a section of coastline you have driven along many times. Perhaps the best way to approach the mysteries of a chart is to set firmly in your mind that it is not a road map. The numbered buoys and land marks may seem to be route markers, but making a right or left turn at Route 295 on land does not depend on where the wind is coming from. What the marks on a chart do is give you reference points to lay out your own "highway," as well as alternates if conditions change. While this requires more attention while sailing, look at it this way: You will never have to sit in your boat waiting until some bored flagger decides to let you pass by a construction site.

Reproduced here is a section of a typical chart. Note that it is a coastal chart, thus there is an unmarked factor—tide—to be taken into account. That aside, most waterways have some form of chart available. The marking references and buoy systems are different for inland lakes and rivers, but that information is available either on the chart itself, or by reading local cruising guides.

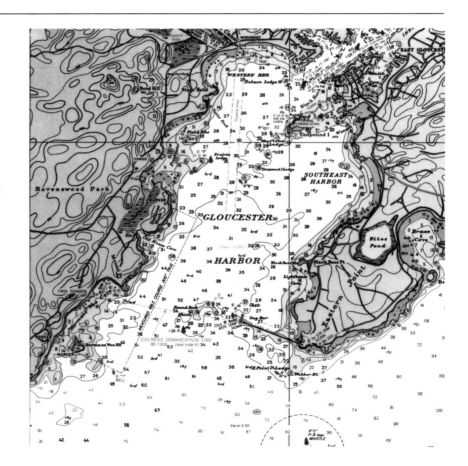

Buoys

These are floating hollow metal structures kept in place by a length of chain running to a heavy weight on the bottom. They may be conical, can, or light-tower shaped depending on purpose, and could also contain lights, whistles, or horns. Buoys mark channels, underwater hazards, or harbor approaches. They are identified on the charts by color, type, and what form, if any, of visual or audio warning device they carry. They are also numbered and sometimes lettered so you can distinguish between several of the same type that may be in close proximity—though those numbers are only sequential within a small range. There may be an "A-7" in one location as part of a sequence and another just four miles up the coast, so coming out of a thick fog upon "A-7" might not mean you know just where you are without other references.

Soundings

Charts are read not only north, south, east, and west, but vertically as well. The soundings shown on charts are, in the case of tidal waters, taken at mean low water—the average depth at a given spot when the tide is fully out. Since on the full moon the tide is stronger than in the last quarter, the tide may be a foot or more lower; it is best to allow a margin of a foot or more to those readings.

Since most beachcruisers and all rowing and powerboats in this class draw very little water—some only inches—why worry about depth? In very calm waters perhaps you would worry very little—save for the chance of damaging a propeller or banging up a keel or centerboard if you are a little off in your navigating. But "thin" water can be very tricky in heavier conditions. Fifteen knots of wind affects water at 10 feet differently than it does at 10 fathoms. The deeper water has more room to absorb the wave action and produces a longer, easier motion. The same waves in short ground tend to be choppy, steep and can produce a very unsteady motion in a small light boat. Also, since shallow water tends to be near land, trying to sail close in heavy air leaves you little sea room, especially if the wind is onshore. Winds around headlands, banks, and ledges tend to be fluky—changing direction often as they bounce off land masses, or going flat just when you need them. You can see how what looks like just statistical information on a chart, when coupled with actual weather conditions, can become very important "live" data.

Another use in reading soundings—in either coastal or river conditions—is to assess their effect on tide and current; both tend to run faster over shallow ground. If, for example, you are approaching a narrows against the flow and making three knots under sail alone, you might find

Primary Navigation Chart Symbols

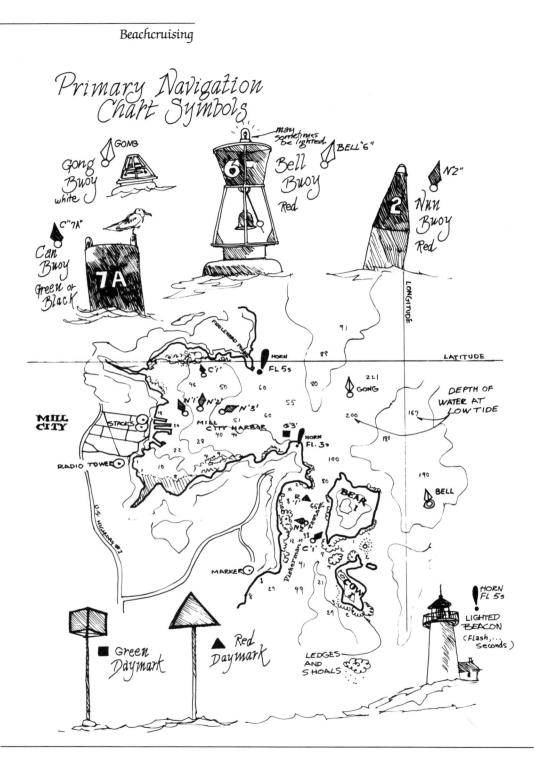

Gong Buoy
white

GONG

C"7A"

Can Buoy
Green or Black

7A

may sometimes be lighted.

6

BELL"6"

Bell Buoy
Red

N"2"

2

Nun Buoy
Red

LONGITUDE

91

FIDDLEHEAD RIVER

HORN
FL 5s

C"1"

89

LATITUDE

46   50   60

80

221

GONG

DEPTH OF
WATER AT
LOW TIDE

N"1" N"2"

N"3"

55

MILL
CITY

STACKS

MILL
CITY HARBOR

51

60

G"3"

200

167

HORN
FL. 3s

RADIO TOWER

MARKER

40

28

22

10

100

190

BELL

R

BEAR
I.

80

65

180

N"2"

C"1"

COW

LEDGES
AND
SHOALS

HORN
FL 5s

LIGHTED BEACON
(Flash,...
Seconds.)

Green
Daymark

Red
Daymark

82

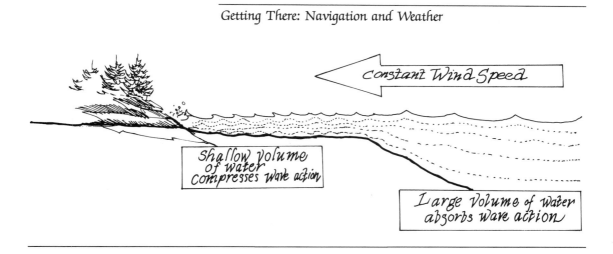

yourself nearly stopped as you approach the shallows—meaning you'd either have to abandon course or use auxiliary power to get through. Naturally, a narrow passage, even if it's in deep water, has the same effect on current.

When negotiating a river, even under power, if you keep toward the banks going upstream, the current is less. Conversely, you can get a free lift downstream by riding the main flow in the middle. Both coastal and river currents are significant forces, though they may not be readily apparent. The effect is most dramatic on a rower, who might find himself "rowing in place" if he has not judged the strength of the current. Yet even a powered craft can learn to take advantage of tidal and river currents—if for no other reason than to save fuel.

OTHER NAVIGATION MARKS

When asked to define a navigation aid, every landlubber in the country would probably say, "A lighthouse, of course." They are picturesque, valuable to the offshore mariner, and can be seen from a greater distance than a buoy, but they generally aren't common enough to become a standard part of your beachcruising navigation; and except on the larger lakes and rivers, they don't exist inland. They are certainly a good reference point, but you aren't likely to close with one as fast as a freighter, so the smaller points of reference are probably more useful. I'd class lighthouses, for our purposes, with such other highly visible landmarks as radio towers and smokestacks.

Daymarks are triangular beacons, usually bright green or red, depending on which side of the channel they mark, fixed atop a ledge, and warn of underwater obstructions. The chart will tell you in which direction the submerged obstruction lies, but it's generally a good idea to sail wide of the whole area.

One of the most frequently used aids to navigation is the shape of surrounding terrain, but it isn't without its pitfalls. "That's Cobble Island — right there ahead. See Beatrice? You can tell because it's higher on this end — just like it shows on the chart!" So you keep sailing toward it, wondering what that other island off to the starboard is — since it isn't on the chart. All of a sudden Beatrice asks nicely, "Why is Cobble Island called an island if it's connected by that road over there to the mainland?" Hmmmmm.

This phenomenon is not limited only to First Time Frank. I've sailed Penobscot Bay for years, but under certain conditions of light, haze, or fog, I have completely mistaken one familiar land mass for another. The shore line on the horizon often can appear to be an island, and there is, under glassy seas or the right refraction of light, a mirage-like phenomenon that makes large ships or land masses appear taller than they are. The point of all this is that unless a land mass has a known mark, such as the picturesque lighthouse, or until you are *very* familiar with your local waters, the "shape" of islands and headlands are not necessarily reliable marks for navigation.

Here's another example. Having made the decision to anchor for the night in a clearly marked and inviting cove on an island that you have yet to visit, you make course for where the cove is supposed to be. But approaching, you don't see it, and fearing crashing on the ledges that are in sight, you veer off, only to feel foolish when suddenly there it is. On re-examination of the chart it was just your relative position that caused your concern. As far as I know, very few islands or coves have moved much in the last few centuries, but no mariner is ever completely immune from the temporary assertion that they have. Ultimately you have to begin to trust your charts, and even more so, the next aid to navigation—the compass.

ABOUT COMPASSES

It doesn't really make much difference if you buy name-brand boat shoes or less expensive but essentially similar copies, but don't stint on your compass. For small boats, you'd never have to spend more than $100, and probably less, but go with known names like Ritchie, Danforth, or Airguide, and get one appropriate to your boat. A powerboat compass and a sailing compass are not the same; they have different compensating systems to correct errors—especially in the case of the stronger electrical interference prevalent on powerboats. If you are going to rely on your compass (and you are going to rely on your compass) you need to know it was built properly in the first place.

If you look on your chart, you will see, usually in two or three places, a compass rose. You will notice that the outer circle indicates true north, the inner one magnetic north—with a difference of 15-20 degrees. As most of us know from school days, the earth's magnetic field causes the mechanical compass needle to swing, but the amount varies the farther north or south you are from the equator. Therefore a compass should be adjusted for local error. All good compasses come with correcting magnets, a non-magnetic tool for adjusting them, and clear instructions for doing this. Even for a small boat this is worth doing. On a bright day you can "compensate" by eye; in darkness or fog, the compass rose on your chart is of little value without knowing the actual deviation in your compass.

Mount your compass in an easily visible location, on the centerline of the hull, away from masses of metal or electrical junction boxes. Any number of things can disturb its accuracy. One common culprit is a portable radio—something that is very likely to be placed in the vicinity of the compass. Its speakers have magnets around them; your course for Block

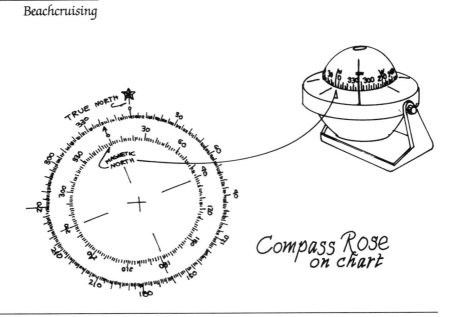

Compass Rose
on chart

Island might turn out to be for Port-Au-Prince. Can openers, metal sun-glasses, knives, all can conspire to lead you astray. Beware.

You can do all your coastal navigating with one fixed compass, but since taking land bearings is an integral part of this art, it's none too convenient to scrunch down trying to sight across it to take a bearing. A hand-bearing compass with a pelorus (a sight gauge, something like a gunsight) is very handy for this chore.

Guidebooks

If you are new to this kind of cruising, or unfamiliar with the area you are about to sail, it would be nice to have an old hand aboard who is intimately familiar with the local currents, points of interest, and that uncharted rock. If you know someone like that, invite them along for an afternoon if you can. But if you don't, the next best aid to navigation is the cruising guidebook. As a testament to the popularity of recreational cruising, a growing number of books are being written by experienced sailors who are familiar with their particular regions—both coastal and inland waterways—who want to share their hard-won information with others. Naturally there is a range of information—some seem to be generally confined to where to buy ice, gas, and which marina to tie up to, but

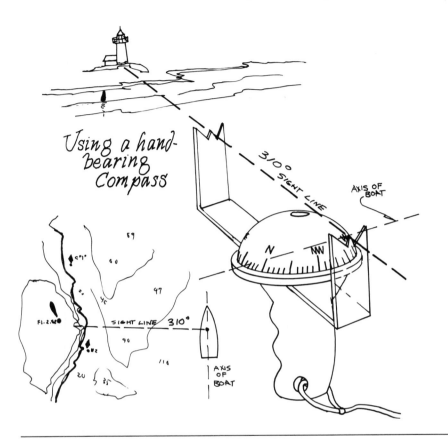

Using a hand-bearing Compass

the better ones have a wealth of topographical, local weather, flora and fauna, local hazards, anchoring and access information as well. There is a listing of some of these published guides in the sources section of this book, but I'd like to quote from my friends Hank and Jan Taft's *A Cruising Guide to the Maine Coast* (International Marine Publishing 1988; Second Edition, 1991):

> Pleasant Point Gut is a working harbor on the west side of the entrance to the St. George River, north of Gay Island. It offers extremely good protection under almost any conditions, and the current through the gut is not strong. People who were born here know how to get through the western entrance to the Gut safely at high water, but this is not recommended for strangers. The western entrance dries out a couple of hours before low tide.

APPROACHES: The best time to enter is at dead low tide, from the east, so the ledge making out from tiny Flea Island (unnamed on the chart) midway through the Gut, is visible. Note that can "5" is a river marker, not a harbor buoy, and you leave it to starboard on entering the Gut. After rounding the northern tip of Gay Island, favor the northern shore of the Gut. The major danger is the ledge making out north and northeast of Flea Island, which is about the same length as the island itself.

ANCHORAGES, MOORINGS: You may be lucky enough to find an available mooring by asking around, but be prepared to anchor. Drop the hook in 10 to 13 feet of water at low, before you get to Kip's Seafood dock on the north shore. Holding ground is good, in mud, and the harbor offers extremely good protection under most conditions. There is not, however, a great deal of extra room.

This is valuable, detailed information, and their book should be a model for all cruising guides. They often tell, for instance, of sailing up to what appears to be a very attractive island that, on the chart, appears to have a nice anchorage. Upon arrival they discover it is just the opposite, with poor ground and exposed rocks. They might recommend it as a lunch stop, or suggest you avoid it altogether. They did their research over a number of seasons, aboard an auxiliary ketch with deep draft, which means that a shoal-draft boat might venture into slightly thinner waters, but the information remains just as valuable for all mariners. In addition to the necessary boating information, they also include local customs, history, and points of interest—as well as caveats regarding landing on public or private properties—the issue of access that we'll discuss in Chapter 4. Good guidebooks exist for nearly any beachcruising locale; buy one.

An Armchair Cruise

Now that you have a few tools and have begun to familiarize yourself with their meaning, set your chart and compass before you on the table and plan a short excursion. Decide for yourself where the wind is coming from—maybe pencil it in as well as its velocity—and the set of the current or tide if any.

Say you pick an island roughly four miles to the northeast of your starting point. Examine the chart and see if you can determine the best place to land. If you don't have a cruising guide or a friend who has been there, read the depths at the island's perimeter, along with any indications of ledge or rocks. Generally, if there is a series of low depth numbers

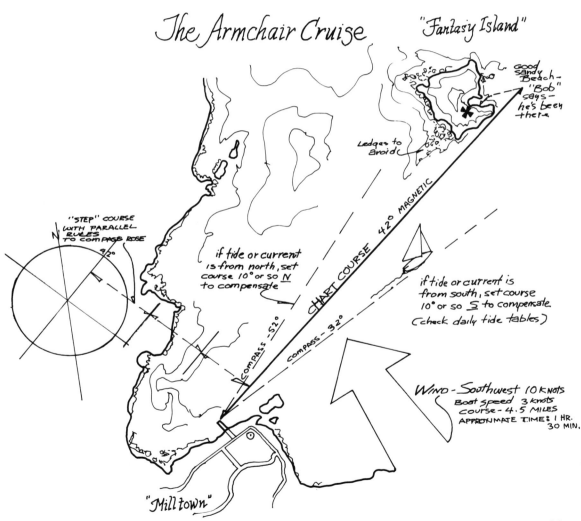

matched with low-lying topography where you want to land (most charts have contour lines), it might prove a suitable landing spot. If not, you may have to explore further. For now let's assume that it is a suitable spot to land, but that it is on the opposite side of the island from your approach. Your course around the island will then be, if sailing, north of it, so you can run down to the site if possible. If conditions are right you might tack by to the south, closing with the site on the return upwind tack.

Either way, run a line from your start to the point nearest the island before going around it. Using your parallel rules, "walk" the line over to the rose, and take your bearing (magnetic), marking it on the line. If the wind is from the southwest and the current from the north, chances are that will be fairly close to your actual course made good, but if both are on the same side, you will have to compensate by sailing higher or lower. Given the data of distance, current, wind speed, and boat speed, this can be calculated, but for our purposes, this will be by observation.

In your living room, of course, conditions can be just as you like, but out on the water, you can determine course drift by lining up with your compass course and then watching your wake: If it angles away from your course to the north then you are being set south, and so on. You can also do this by taking back bearings: You were sailing 60 degrees NE and your launch site was in a direct line with your island, but after a half hour, looking back, it is well off to port. You're being set south and have to sail higher to compensate.

If you know the approximate speed of your boat under the conditions you have set on paper, you can estimate the arrival time. This of course is an ultra-simple cruise, but by walking through it you can now lay out more complicated zigs and zags—taking in a few headlands, sunken pirate ships, foul tides, contrary winds, and sudden squalls. You could even have a spirited game of "what if" right on your card table; lighthearted as it may seem, it will set your thought process in motion for more-real circumstances. And if you are ready for an actual cruise, the time spent laying it out at home will be well worth it—especially if conditions or destinations change en route.

I stress planning and patience—even if these factors seem to run contrary to that free-spirited adventure I keep promising you. Well, running the Snowmass at Aspen on a glorious April day must be pure heaven, free as a bird, but not if you don't know how to ski. Become skilled at coastal piloting and you will go wherever you want with freedom and confidence.

There is more to navigation than this, of course, even for coastal piloting, but I'd like to introduce at this time the element that makes navigation necessary at all in small boats—weather.

Weather

We are so used to getting our information from remote sources that we probably don't realize how little we know of what is behind that data. We hear weather reports, stock market reports, and world events, and based on experience and conditioning we just react—adjusting for what we perceive as being important to our daily lives. In truth, there is so much information to process in this day and age that we have little other choice most of the time. Since the activity we're espousing in this book is intended to be a little outside the mainstream, there are some opportunities for getting the information we need right from the source—in this case nature.

I don't mean to imply that when contemplating an outing you shouldn't consult your local weather broadcasts; the TV news is especially valuable in showing the satellite overview of moving fronts, high and low pressure areas, and temperature gradients. For the mariner, the NOAA (National Oceanographic & Atmospheric Administration) reports are very specific and localized, and provide a general base for making a decision before starting out. A very handy device for this information is the 24-hour weather-only radio broadcast, available any time at the touch of a button (weather radios can be had for around $20 at Radio Shack or the like), and updated by NOAA every six hours. In some locations this same information is available by phone, but I've rarely found the line free.

When you leave the dock in a small boat, you have disconnected yourself from the synthesis of electronic data—even if you are carrying a weather radio with you. It may not seem like a very significant step, given the short range of most excursions, but the process combines the opportunity to be connected more closely with the natural world, with an ability to feel comfortable in it by gaining experience with both navigation and weather. That weather affects navigation is obvious, but by gaining a basic understanding of forecasting it yourself you can make the best use of it—for better cruising and safer navigation.

READING THE SKY

"Red sky at night, sailors' delight, red sky in the morning, sailors take warning."

"There is a ridge of high pressure just along the eastern side of the White Mountains, with a warm front moving behind it from the west—an offshore low seems to be moving to the northeast, with temperatures along the coast expected in the mid-70s. Now today in sports, the Chicago Cubs dropped another one. . . ."

Old sea lore and modern data processing—but with much the same information. The "ancient mariners" couldn't fly high to see the weather patterns, but they could read the signs well enough to know generally what was coming. As a casual mariner, you can use the best of both sources, and a good way to begin is to familiarize yourself with a few basic cloud types and formations. It's interesting to note that the TV satellite pictures can always tell you where the clouds are, but not what type, unless you are an experienced meteorologist.

Major Cloud Formations	Weather Usually Associated with Them
High Clouds	
Cirrus	In quantity, a sign of deteriorating weather
Cirrocumulus	Wave-like cirrus clouds—same effect
Cirrostratus	Thin veil of cirrus clouds, sun is barely visible—onset of bad weather
Middle Clouds	
Alto Cumulus	"Mackerel" sky—indicates change
Alto	The classic "gray skies," light rain, but generally mild weather
Nimbostratus	More shape—rain carrying clouds
Low Clouds	
Stratocumulus Cumulus	Soft, shapeless dull-day type, usually without precipitation. Sky "fog"—generally recedes with the sun and heat
Larger Clouds	
Stratocumulus	Towering, very picturesque, associated with approaching cold fronts and thunderstorms
Cumulus	The small puffy ones—fine weather—though they bear watching—when they "gang up" they may form stratocumulus

The type of cloud does not necessarily guarantee a specific result. Much has to do with time of year, wind speed and direction, and your distance from land. It takes experience and local knowledge to produce finite forecasts from clouds, but by knowing the general types you know what is possible—and by connecting what you see before you with wind speed and direction as well as your official electronic forecast—you can decide where, in what direction, and how far you may wish to sail.

If you are already on the water and see an approaching front, knowing the type of weather it is likely to bring can help you can determine your safety margin and consider alternate courses.

This would be a good time to emphasize a common occurence—and a potentially dangerous one for small craft. Being out in rainy or moderately windy weather does not have to be threatening. Sometimes a front approaching in the right direction can give you a good "sleigh ride" if you are prepared for it, but when a strong front from one direction strikes a sea running in the opposite, a short, choppy, and sometimes confused wave action results. It might be nothing but a nuisance to a 600-foot freighter, but it's an event that could, if misjudged, capsize a small sail or powerboat. I'd have to say that sailors generally tend to be more cautious by nature in such conditions. Having power at your disposal sometimes gives one the false confidence that you can motor your way out of trouble. It ain't necessarily so. When such conditions begin to appear, try to get into sheltered waters as soon as possible.

SEVERE WEATHER

While we are on the doom and gloom kick, let's deal with the worst of it. Two rules: when not to go out at all, and what to do if you are caught out in threatening weather. If there is a small red flag displayed at your marina, Coast Guard Station, or Yacht Club, or if the reports contain the words, "Small Craft Warnings," *stay home*! If there are two flags flying, stay home twice as hard. You may see commercial fisherman steaming right past the warning flags, but they go out because they have to—and you don't.

Nonetheless, sometimes weather makes over you faster than you are capable of avoiding it, though another old saw holds that, "Slow to strike, long to last—Quick to come, soon past". This doesn't apply to gales and hurricanes of course, but occasionally you may get caught out in a line squall or a thunderstorm. If under sail, get all sail down, secure loose gear, and if you have plenty of sea room, just try to keep her headed slightly into the wind. Most proper boats will take care of themselves if you let them.

If you are near a threatening headland or some rocky ground, try to bear off slightly with either a heavily reefed main or just the scrap of a jib. In a powerboat, you can use the engine to effect the same procedure—either just maintaining steerage or bearing off slightly if you have to stay clear of obstructions. Naturally everyone should don life jackets, and have any other safety equipment close to hand.

If there is lightning with the storm, go below if you can, or get as far down in the boat as possible, and don't touch metal surfaces if you can avoid it. If you must leave the helm, tie it off to try to keep position. With a sailboat you can heave to: that is, back the jib to windward, and tie the tiller in the opposite direction; this will keep the boat weather cocked, which should keep it from broaching.

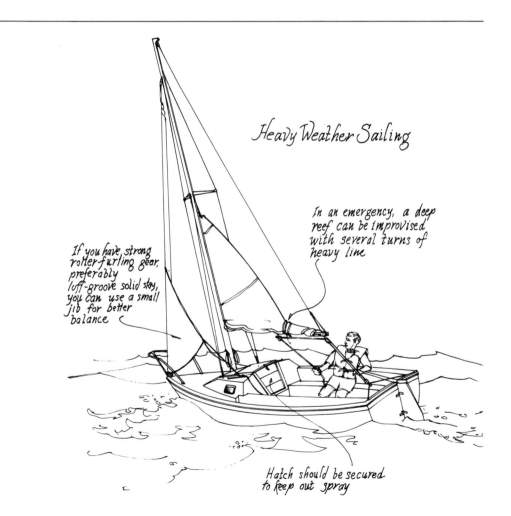

Heavy Weather Sailing

In an emergency, a deep reef can be improvised with several turns of heavy line

If you have strong roller-furling gear, preferably luff-groove solid stay, you can use a small jib for better balance

Hatch should be secured to keep out spray

In any event, stay with the boat unless it is in imminent danger of sinking. Survival in sea conditions is chancy at any season; hypothermia, even in summer, can render you helpless in the water in a surprisingly brief time. Don't panic. Focus on activities rather than speculations. Of course that's easier said than done, but it may well save your life.

After all that I think it's time to let the squall pass and the sun come out, and let us get back to the pleasures of navigation and weather, rather than dwelling on the discomforts of their fouler side.

Turnabout is fair play. If the weather can mess up your well-laid plans you can, in turn, learn to take advantage of its phenomena. Since you will most likely be boating near a coastline or land mass of some form, you can learn to use the sea-breeze–land-breeze pattern. In coastal areas and on larger lakes, as the sun rises in the morning and heats up the land inshore, a thermal updraft of warm air is created, leaving behind a vacuum underneath. Cooler air is drawn in from the surface of the water, and this in turn is warmed over the land and rises, too.

This flow is called a sea breeze, constantly drawn in over land from offshore during the warm hours of daylight. You can use a sea breeze to your advantage when you are offshore and the wind slackens. By heading inshore, you will generally find the wind is strongest as you close with the land—you might consider making several short tacks alongshore to gain your objective. However, since wind follows whatever it bumps into, be prepared for changes as you traverse a high headland or a long, low stretch of land.

This type of air flow, especially in summer when the land is hottest, tends to peak in late afternoon. As the air cools, the breeze slackens; the procedure is reversed overnight, often giving you a land breeze in the early morning—which is very useful when heading out. Naturally this particular phenomenon ties in with the multiplicity of other conditions—which is why more time spent on the water can increase your sailing skills. With experience you will know how to interpret the weather and get the most good sailing out of it.

This brings us to one final phenomenon (excluding winter conditions, which I assume few of us will be considering for beachcruising expeditions, at least in northern climes): The great and gray *fog*! I don't classify it as precisely a hazard, (which of course it can be), or necessarily impossible to cope with. The point is, fog does occur, in virtually all waterways at one time or another. You can't readily park the boat and take the bus home, so it might be worth knowing a little about how to navigate in it.

I could explain how fog is formed, but that won't help you much: Sometimes you can predict it and sometimes you can't. Often you can see it coming, though—and there is your first line of defense. When you see fog forming, plot your position *now* so you have some reference when you lose visual contact with your marks. If you plan to continue your course, what headings will you need? And what marks do you think you can find by dead reckoning?

Lay a compass course, allow for current and wind and, despite that funny feeling on the back of your neck (which is probably just the damp), *trust your compass*. You may think your instincts will tell you where you are going but they will not, unless you are a fisherman who has plied these waters all his life and can navigate by sea swell, smell, sound, and the color of the water.

You need your ears to listen for sound buoys and fog horns. Take their bearings and stay the course on the chart as best you can: You can't trust your ears completely; sound distorts in fog, especially if there is a wind against you.

I once ran some 40 miles in a fog along the Maine coast, navigating from buoy to buoy, headed for a huge foghorn on Seguin at the mouth of

the Kennebec River. My log showed me I should have been there but there was not a sound as I approached; the wind was blowing from the southwest. All of a sudden I saw large rocks ahead and assumed I was about to crash into the coast, when I heard the feeble bleating of the horn. It was not until I looked up that I realized I was at Seguin Island. Rounding it to seaward, the noise grew almost deafening. My fog run had been rewarding, though. I had sharpened my piloting skills a little, and for the payoff, as I headed upriver the sun broke through and we made anchorage on a sunny, peaceful note.

If you are in an area of expected traffic, use a portable foghorn to warn others of your presence, and listen for theirs. If your chart shows a commercial traffic lane, get to one side or the other of it as quickly as possible; a large ship might pick you up on radar, but it takes most of them a mile or so to stop and a good distance to alter course. Right of way is not an issue—safety is.

Assuming you don't have radar and you have decided to try your luck at fog running, another way to cross-check your bearings if you can't find sufficient buoys or other landmarks is to use soundings. While I promote the notion of simplicity in small boat cruising, there are some handy electronics available at reasonable investment. One is the digital depth sounder. By running a pencil line on the chart over your intended course, you can read the soundings along it as you proceed, and if you begin to stray, you can tell in which general direction by following the deviation of depth readings. Even if you do not have an electronic sounder you can use a lead line—a length of chord with a lead weight at one end, and either fathom or foot markings at appropriate intervals. This is slower, but it has worked for centuries.

I have given you just an overview of the arts of navigation and weather sense, along with, I hope, some practical applications for small-boat cruising. Because we are talking about a flexible agenda in beach-cruising, most of the unpleasant or difficult aspects of both can be avoided by good planning and picking your weather, but the more experienced you become at handling your boat under a variety of conditions, the greater your freedom to use it will become.

And if you are forced to "hole up" somewhere, perhaps in an island cove, use the experience to watch the more interesting effects of a day of foul weather. Observe how the birds and animals react, see the colors and patterns of the sky and the waves. You can see it all in a much different perspective from this vantage point. And as usual in most seasonal boating weather, the following day will bring a return to clear skies, and a satisfying, and probably thoughtful ride home.

CHAPTER Four

The Marine Environment: Use, Access, and Conservation

It is one of those rare fine mornings in Maine. As if by design a gentle northwest wind ripples the riverway in front of my home. The boat is ready on the shore; I have but to carry my cooler aboard, raise sail, and slip downwind toward Port Clyde and the island as the July sun slowly lights the western shoreline. Deep stands of fir and spruce line the St. George River, and I've never traveled its length without seeing at least one seal. Often there are loons, cormorants (always cormorants, alternating between drying their wings in comic poses and expertly diving for breakfast), and if one is lucky a heron or even an eagle. With a Sibelius symphony on the radio accompanied by a thick cup of coffee from my thermos, I have a grand sense of peace and deep happiness.

By eleven I'm tied up at the busy fishing village of Port Clyde. Though the population of us summer sailors is growing along the coast, it's refreshing to spend time among a different people—those who have for generations experienced a strong and natural bond with the sea. The area abounds with lobstermen, clam diggers, scallop draggers. If one maintains a respectful distance, an easy, friendly relationship generally exists between working fishermen and we recreational sea dabblers.

Mankind's "Gifts" to the Sea.

After lunch I make out past Hooper Island to the southwest, planning to find a little cove at Thompson; I've heard there are wild sheep there and I'd like to see them. This island has a rugged, wild beauty about it. Surrounding ledges discourage access, and the small gravel beach is the only possibility, but my lightweight, flat-bottomed sharpie is easily pulled up on the shelf. From a distance I see one or two sheep walking along, silhouetted against the thick evergreen forest blanketing the high ground. I close with the shore, still lost in a reverie sweetened by the fine day and the sights and smells of the sea.

The approach is tricky, and it occupies my attention as I close with the shore. Once made and the boat secured, I turn to climb the steep granite to the island turf, but I'm stopped dead. Plastic oil containers, discarded Pampers, cans, liquor bottles, rusty scrap metal, bits of pot warp, old boots, gloves, endless Styrofoam, fast food containers—the effluence of affluence litters the rocky shoreline. I've always had a habit of picking up the odd bit of debris or garbage I find along shore, but to cart off what I saw before me on Thompson Island, just two miles out in the sparkling Atlantic, I'd need a barge! Who could have put all this stuff here?

Who?

Sadly, all of us: Lobstermen, sailors, mothers of small children, children themselves who haven't been taught not to—and though I hope I've become aware enough to know better—maybe even me, by remaining silent when I see such transgressions take place.

I've always thought of Maine as being remote, out of the mainstream, but the polluted mainstream has become much broader of late, and the evidence of man's carelessness can be found hundreds of miles from civilization: in the Arctic, in mid-ocean, in outer space—we've managed to introduce our trash to areas where we ourselves have never been.

Most of our information comes from the media—and right now environmental issues are hot press—yet the media are synthetic and fickle. There is enough air and abstraction between it and us to temper our well-intended response to a global problem until the moment passes and another issue takes its place.

I don't intend to become heavy-handed and preachy in a book celebrating freestyle cruising, yet we cannot isolate ourselves from the issue even in our private recreation—perhaps especially in our private recreation: We owe our pleasure to the very waterways we seem bent on destroying. I don't propose that every beachcruiser turn privateer and start ramming polluters, but by *not* being part of the problem, we may at least begin to be part of the solution.

There is a bumper sticker that reads "Think Globally, Act Locally." This is how the job gets done. After all, that's how most of the garbage got on the shore in the first place—one handful at a time. I am no militant marcher nor, I suspect, are most of you. And while redressing global wrongs takes the dramatic and brave actions of activists, their efforts are ultimately meaningless unless we adjust our thinking and that of our children to automatically do the right thing.

It isn't just a matter of carelessly discarded waste. In the marine environment there are many issues to consider: conservation of wildlife, both flora and fauna; water quality; protecting eroding shorelines from the wakes of high-powered boats or the unthinking defoliation of developers; balancing the needs of commerce, recreation, and habitat; private waterfront development versus public usage—and the complex relationships of all of the above.

There is a tendency for some environmental groups to want to surround threatened areas, declaring hands off—and in some cases the abuse has been substantial enough to warrant it. But in the give and take of human relationships, often a dialog between a variety of interests can produce a workable compromise between conservation and development.

In the spirit of "acting locally," in Maine we have an organization known as the Island Institute, formed to act as a catalyst—not as a spokesman for one specific concern—between the wide and often conflicting spectrum of uses, needs, and ownerships of more than 3,000 islands along the coast.

In *A Cruising Guide to the Maine Coast,* Hank Taft wrote: "The purpose of the Institute is to see whether there are practical and economic ways to use Maine islands today—rather than abandon them entirely to nature or the onslaught of vacation homes."

A case in point are the sheep I came to see on Thompson Island. There, the grazing flock is wild and untended, but on nearby Allen Island is a domestic population put there in the same manner as was common a hundred years ago. When the Allen Island project was undertaken, an uninformed passerby might have expressed dismay at seeing one end of the island being clear-cut of trees—though its purpose was to create pasture land, not to profit a pulpwood cutter.

All along the coast, islands are being logged, farmed, and quarried again—though responsibly and with an eye toward preserving their natural cycle. In areas where the preservation of wildlife habitat is critical, the Institute and other organizations are active in their management. In some cases the islands are purchased through land trusts, in others they are either leased or managed with the consent of their owners.

Within the Island Institute is an association of particular interest to the boating public. The Maine Island Trail Association has established a growing "trail" of public and private islands available for use by its members. A sort of waterborne Appalachian Trail, it provides an interesting and varied tour, especially designed for access by small craft. The association publishes a comprehensive and frequently updated guidebook, and has an "adopt an Island" policy that provides a stewardship for individual members to monitor and help preserve and protect a particular island's ecology. A side benefit of this has been that many private islands, not previously open for public use, have been "leased" to the Trail. And provided its members do not abuse the privilege, these additions offer the opportunity to explore many new and fascinating places.

Similar groups in Seattle, Boston, and Georgia are good examples of bringing environmental needs into focus, inviting participation by local residents and visitors, and offering something in return—information and assistance in planning and enjoying a waterborne excursion. One needn't be a flag-waving causeur to participate, but by becoming aware and involved, "act locally" becomes more than a bumper-sticker slogan.

If you look around you may well find similar efforts underway in your own waterways. If you don't, consider starting one.

So much for the structure and philosophy of environmental concerns. What about realistic and practical guidelines for the individual? The following advice is adapted from the Island Trail Association's handbook, and it provides a balanced approach to waterway use that is applicable nearly anywhere:

WELCOME TO RAM ISLAND
PLEASE ENJOY THE ISLAND, AND
RESPECT ITS ENVIRONMENT.
NO FIRES, DUMPING OR LITTER.
THIS IS PRIVATE PROPERTY MADE
AVAILABLE FOR YOUR RESPONSIBLE
USE BY MAINE ISLAND TRAIL ASSOC.

- If the ecosystems of the islands are undisturbed today, it is the responsibility of any of those who visit them to leave them in the same condition. If we think of ourselves as guests when we are using the islands we can't go too far wrong.
- Soils are the most fragile living things on an island. Once lost, a single inch of new organic material can take centuries, and in some extreme cases, 1,000 years, to be replaced. Our greatest impact on island soils almost always occurs when we go ashore. When you are scrambling onto an island, find a point where the shore is stable, avoiding places where the soil is already exposed. It is better to walk over spreading mats of vegetation that cushion your arrival than over loose dirt.
- On an island the only safe place for a fire is on the shore below the storm high-tide mark. If you must have a fire, it's best to carry a steel pan of some sort (a garbage can cover works well) and build your fire in that so you don't mark any rocks. Otherwise, line the fire area with small stones that can be thrown into the water before you leave; this will keep larger rocks and ledges from becoming shattered and blackened by fire. Use only driftwood for firewood; the thin island soils need all the standing and fallen deadwood for revitalization. The best way to avoid all this is to use a camp stove.

103

- In this day of weightless garbage bags, rubbish should never be a problem for island campers. Even kayakers can compact their trash into small bundles that can be stowed in their boats. Paper rubbish can be burned, but plastic, glass, and metals should be taken ashore for proper disposal.
- Grass is an amazingly resilient ground cover and will support moderate to heavy traffic without much damage. By contrast, spruce, fir, and pine needles form but a thin cover over vulnerable root systems.
- Pets and wildlife don't mix. You will do yourself, others, and the island a big favor by leaving your pets on the mainland. On small islands especially, wildlife is vulnerable to harassment by pets, and a dog can wipe out a bird's production for an entire year in a few joyous seconds.

Where to Go

What sort of waterways make good small-boat cruising? On the face of it, anyplace that looks appealing—at least from the standpoint of adventure, scenery, and variety. Only the size and nature of your craft will limit you—certainly one wouldn't want to try to cross the Columbia Bar in a daysailer or risk being run over by a barge on the Mississippi River in a rowboat, but common sense and a little inquiry into local conditions will tell you where an appropriate waterway might be. I'd recommend the more remote, unvisited spots rather than rivers or lakes or bays crowded with traffic and expensive marinas. Get out an atlas, look at an area you are interested in, and perhaps focus on, say, a major bay and trace some of its backwaters. The Neuse River off Pamlico Sound in North Carolina comes to mind—it snakes all over the place and leads to some unspoiled areas perfect for shallow-draft boats. A phone call or letter to either state or local chambers of commerce, or departments of fisheries and inland waterways, will generally yield a wealth of local information about launching ramps, climate, currents, best seasons to travel, and the like.

Before you can get to an island, beach, or backwater, you first have to get in the water, and for a majority of beachcruisers, home port is the family garage or backyard, and the mooring is a trailer. The obvious advantage to trailering is that it widens the cruising range dramatically and makes available a vast array of choices: For a day trip it may be a spot just a bit farther up the coast than you can sail in a day; for the weekend it may be an inland lake 50 miles away that you've never visited; for a vacation it might be the other side of the country.

I say this is obvious, but Larry Brown, perhaps the best-known trailer sailor in the country, says in his book *Sailing America:* "We found no one doing what we were doing, and I'm convinced that there are far more people circumnavigating the globe than there are circumnavigating America with a boat in tow. That's ironic, since most people can't really pull up stakes and go sailing around the planet, but almost anyone can do what we've been doing—in smaller increments if not all at once."

Perhaps most of us will never cover as many road and water miles as Larry Brown and his West Wight Potter *Fearless,* but his point is well taken: The possibilities are greater than we imagine. I'd be willing to bet that, not unlike the fatcat marina cruisers used only for cocktail parties, the majority of trailerable boats don't go much farther over the road than their local launch site—despite the fact that there is a whole continent out there for the cruising, at 55 miles per hour dead to windward.

Most of us like a good adventure and thoughts of faraway places; many dream of the ultimate voyage across exotic waters to unspoiled is-

lands. Larry Brown is right when be observes that there are more blue-water cruisers than ever, but bluewater cruising requires a huge commitment of time and resources, and certainly entails more risk. Having done a fair amount of offshore sailing, I can tell you that getting there is not always a grand experience. The ocean can be by turns awe-inspiring, exhausting, and boring. For some the offshore environment is home—they feel ill at ease in port. For many it quickly becomes an obstacle between you and your destination.

Given the interstate highway system, you can make the outward-bound leg of a voyage quickly, skipping over whatever distances you choose to get to the landscape further in. A boater from Kansas may want to cruise and fish Lake Superior; a family from sunny Georgia may want to tour the foggy coast of Maine; a frozen Minnesotan may be drawn by Florida Bay; a jaded New Yorker may want to lose himself in Kentucky's Land Between the Lakes.

You can make your northing, easting, or westing rather quickly on the interstate, but don't limit yourself to that. Go shunpiking some distance from your intended launch site; allow yourself to be distracted by whim or whimsy. Get out of the mainstream before you back the trailer into the water. Get into the hinterland, look over the maps, and slow your arrival, savoring the countryside on the way. Forget Holiday Inns and Burger Kings—you have brought your accommodations along. You might spend a memorable night on an anonymous river island you spy in your rear-view mirror just as you see a serendipitous sign pointing the way to a public launching ramp. And just because your boat isn't in the water doesn't mean you can't sleep in it (though you should reserve this, sadly, until you are well into the country or in a well protected, well-lit spot, hopefully with other campers nearby).

Of course it isn't necessary to go transcontinental to find exciting places to cruise. Personally, I'm an advocate of developing an intimate relationship with the marine environment in one's own backyard, though admittedly my backyard borders a coast that provides beauty and infinite variety without having to go more than 20 miles in either direction. However, it isn't necessary to have the Maine coast for a backyard to have quality beachcruising readily to hand.

I spent many years in Boston, whose harbor offers a few snug coves to explore even in the midst of the industrial and commercial activity. An hour's sail got me out to Bumpkin or Georges or some other outer harbor island, rich with history and rarely visited. If the tour boats of summer weren't rolling by, disco music blasting from their "promenade" deck filled with writhing dancers oblivious to the marine environment, then I might enjoy a peaceful sunset, a simple meal, and wake up surrounded by shore birds and seals rather than bus horns and garbage trucks.

Cruising grounds can be found everywhere, even in the shadows of urban spires. It's a matter of looking for it, and going out to experience it rather than assuming it isn't there.

ON TRAILERING

If you are going into the wilderness with a trailer, make sure you have a good spare wheel and tire, a jack, and a lug wrench. Trailer wheels are smaller and turn twice as fast as your car's wheels, and so are subject to earlier failure. And before you leave home, make sure your equipment is in good order. It may have been sitting for months, the tires' sidewalls gradually weakening and the bearings slowly rusting. Additionally, trailer wheel bearings should be protected by "Bearing Buddies," which allow you to grease the wheel bearings quickly and easily after each use, thus extending their life and warding off problems on the road from overheating bearings. Any marine store dealing in trailers and most auto-parts stores can sell you a set of easily installed Bearing Buddies.

Be cautious if you're buying a used trailer. In areas of salt water, if it has not been washed down with fresh water after *every* use, that trailer may be quietly rusting away—even under that hastily applied coat of silver paint. Be sure, too, that it has been rated for a few hundred pounds of carrying capacity beyond the basic weight of your boat and rig. If your suspension has no reservoirs of strength, a hard bounce could shatter an axle or break a wheel bearing—miles from a garage or water.

While the competition for waterfront space among development, commercial, public, and private interests has severely limited launching sites in many areas, most areas have state, county, and municipal facilities available. A quick phone call (let your fingers do the walking) may bring anything from vague directions to a flood of glossy brochures.

If the waterway you wish to cruise seems to have no convenient public launch site nearby, you can sometimes obtain permission to launch from commercial yards and marinas, though understandably, most will ask a fee. If a site along the way appears suitable but is not marked clearly whether or not it is public, be sure to inquire before using it. Generally you'll receive permission, but taking the assumption may close the site to future use.

The ideal launching ramp has sufficient angle to back down the trailer far enough to float the boat off without submerging the tail end of your car. If the ramp is in salt water, you may need to wait for high tide to do this effectively. If it is just a rural gravel incline or a badly designed ramp, a standard trailer may be ineffective, particularly with larger and heavier boats. You might want to consider one with a tilt bed so you don't have to back as far down the incline.

If you plan a "circumnavigation" of a rural lake or bay, see if you can find a local to inform about your intentions and when you intend to return, perhaps asking the local authorities to keep an eye on your vehicle. If your trip is to be a one-way affair, such as a river or a coastwise passage, you'll need to secure transportation back to pick up your trailer. Rural bus service is usually a bit thin, but many of the more remote areas often have logging or mining activity; with a little initiative and friendliness you might arrange a ride with a trucker — and learn a lot about your new cruising area in the process.

Sometimes, just winging it is the best way to go anywhere — if you have a flexible attitude and the time to work around unexpected variations on the plan. It would be wise, though, to investigate an area you intend to cruise — either through a cruising guide, publications, or talking with someone who knows the area. Consider this: Attracted here by a half-remembered magazine article, you launched your boat at the northern end of a long lake, and have just arrived at the southern end after an arduous four-day voyage. The wind was always on the nose, you have been eaten alive by huge mosquitoes, it rained half the time, and the bus to take you back to your car and trailer doesn't run on that route at this time of the year. You complain to a local that you'd just as soon not visit his country again, and wonder how it could have been so highly recommended. He scratches his head and wonders why you are here in June at all. He never even gets his fishing boat out of the shed until July, when the winds are westerly, the bugs gone, and it don't rain hardly a'tall.

Solo, Pas de Deux, or the Whole Gang?

Although we have talked about the size of your vessel, up to now we have forgone talking about the size of your cruising party. While the answer may seem obvious, you might want to consider some aspects of all three of these options.

I am a very happily married man who enjoys a shared interest in coastal and inland cruising with my wife. I have the greater sailing experience, and she the more intimate knowledge of nature — and there are great pleasures and benefits from this companionship on the water. Most of us hope to get to the point where shared experience is the fabric of our contentment, but I've found that part of the value of a relationship comes from the ability to stand alone, and to appreciate self-reliance and self-discovery.

I don't think it's necessary to take an axe and a sack of flour and head into the wilderness with a canoe to benefit from the solo experience. For most of us it's too big a jump out of time and space, and I'm not sure it's relevant anyway—unless we intend to leave behind society altogether. But as you sail, power, or paddle off alone for a day, an overnight, or longer, letting the usual world of everyday commerce shed itself naturally, your focus begins to shift and you will be amazed at what you might find out—both about yourself and your environment.

While it may be therapeutic, and for some even critical, I'm not really talking about a desperation-driven, "I've got to get away from . . ." situation. To me, soloing means a quiet voyage of self-discovery. If you are trying to sail upwind on a less than perfect day, all the while stewing over your job and your social life, the chances are you won't get much out of the experience. Soloing means focusing on what is actually left after divesting yourself of your normal dependency on social interaction, land-based creature comforts, and structured itinerary. There is opportunity to linger—either in distance traveled or time spent observing some aspect of scenery or wildlife that interests you, or perhaps suggests a different line of thought. It doesn't have to be Zen, it might just be plain trolling for trout.

Aloneness is different from loneliness—though I've found that on most solo trips I experience both. Still, I like the self-dependance and the chance to re-examine goals and attitudes. Oddly, I don't see soloing as risk-taking, certainly not on par with sailing across the Pacific in a small boat. Perhaps I'll sail a bit longer or farther than I might otherwise, get a little wetter from salt spray than my mate might enjoy.

On the practical side of soloing, you might want to review your boat and its gear to see that it is set up for singlehanding. Are you used to your partner going forward to drop the jib? Can you anchor alone? Can you safely handle the boat under adverse conditions? A dry run ashore can make a solo trip a much smoother experience.

And even if you really have no itinerary, be sure to file a general trip plan with someone, with an expected return time. An unfortunate accident would be twice as threatening if you know no one will miss you after an appropriate time.

Some options to consider for soloing: Try leaving behind as many of the usual trappings and conveniences of your everyday life as possible — at least for a little while. For instance, take the weather-only radio but leave behind the daily news broadcasts. Get a good book on foraging and pack a few staples, but leave the fast and easy stuff on the shelf. You won't starve for a day or two if you restrict your diet a bit. I don't mean you have to eat nuts and twigs either; there's some good gourmet stuff out there, but you won't look for it if your pantry is full of pre-packaged meals. (More on this in Chapter 5.) Take along a book you've always meant to read but never found the time. And how do you know you can't draw? Did you ever really try? Take along pencil and paper. Sketch a tree or a seabird. Or if you are goal and activity driven, try throwing yourself wholeheartedly into just being a quiet observer. Oddly enough, a little solo cruising might make you a better companion on your next trip with company.

I've noticed a funny thing about two people in a boat. They start off chattering away about land-based things—the boss, the kids, the latest global disaster—but as they draw farther away from land, inevitably there comes a silence, a drifting off (unless they are slamming along at 30 knots in a candyflake bomb, where conversation—or contemplation—is impossible). Unless the stresses of life ashore are unusually pressing, it takes only a short time before the marine environment begins to exert its influence, and communication centers around what is being observed rather than what was, up to now, "important."

To me, this is what beachcruising is all about: Sailing along, whether two or two hundred miles from home, the layers of concern and conditioning slide back, and alone or in company, we begin to soak up the richness of the *real* world, not the way we perceive it sometimes on television or at the movies.

Friendships have time to flesh out, the slower pace of water travel might loosen the knots in a stressed relationship. And together you can observe, compare, and learn more. And love under the stars, on a deserted beach or in a mossy pine grove? I shouldn't have to elaborate on that.

I don't propose that beachcruising is a panacea for problems global or personal; it will be only what you make it. However, it does provide opportunities away from the mainstream, just far enough out of it to lend perspective. As an adult you can make the choice to find a quiet eddy off the cultural mainstream. As a parent you can force that option on your children. But unless they are drawn naturally to nature and counter-current experiences, being dragged along on a boat-camping trip might not be their idea of fun. It is a paradox that children are by nature the more capable of adapting to new experiences, yet the media that target them use peer pressure to ensure they behave like sheep: New ideas, unless officially sanctioned by an advertising campaign, are uncool.

We all hope that we communicate well enough with our children to make shared family outings attractive, and beachcruising certainly can make for wonderful family outings. But don't assume that the fluorescent-garbed, alien-speaking kid with a boom box glued to his or her ear is not a candidate for wilderness tripping. Getting them there might require coaxing and tact—maybe even bribery—but inviting their participation once on board may produce some surprising results.

If, in the interest of safety, you are inclined to play Captain Bligh—issuing a flurry of orders and restrictions—you may well be faced with a sullen crew, intent on mutiny. Sure, safety is important, but it doesn't have to be heavyhanded, any more than an adult has to have his or her hand on the helm to be "in charge." I once taught skiing, and found by experience that adults needed far more instruction to keep from breaking their legs on the slopes than did kids. I'd set some ground rules, of course, but on the bunny slope it's better to let a novice make his or her own mistakes.

On the water, at slower speeds and in mild conditions, turn over the tiller to your youngsters. So what if you get a little off course or you jibe around a bit? They will learn much more quickly and more enjoyably by actually doing than by enduring a lecture on the art and science of seamanship. Common sense is the best guide, and sharing sailing and navigation chores helps the young mariner develop both self-confidence and a sense of prudent seamanship.

Safety afloat is paramount, of course, for the whole crew: life jackets for non-swimmers or smaller children—and for everyone in rough conditions. They needn't be the primitive bulky type associated with slipping from the *Titanic*'s deck as the band plays Nearer My God to Thee. Modern flotation vests are lightweight and trim, and some are pretty cool, even to jaded teenagers.

Ashore, there is time for both shared and solo discovery. Explore together if you like, share what you know, but allow for each to proceed at his own pace. Don't prohibit *all* electronic diversions; social decorum might eliminate boom boxes, but a Walkman might work. If I feel my nature walk enhanced by Ravel or Debussy, who's to say someone else can't profit emotionally from watching seabirds while listening to the Red Hot Chili Peppers. Lighten up. After awhile the contents of a tidal pool might prove more interesting than the stuff of teen magazines—at least while you are out there, away from the mainstream.

One thing is guaranteed: The kids aren't on the phone—and neither are you. There is time for real communication. There also is time to make issues real. Environmental concerns become tangible when the trash on the beach, or the interaction of a feathered family, is *real,* not just pictures on TV.

A Schoonerman's Breakfast

114

CHAPTER Five

Cruising Cuisine—The Good Life Afloat

It is first light on the Grand Banks of the North Atlantic. The schooner lays to her anchor as the crew awakens. Before swinging their dories over the side for an arduous day trawling for cod, they crowd around the narrow table in the fo'c's'le for a hot breakfast. Breakfast? Baked beans, fish cakes, porridge, potatoes, ham, thick slices of fresh-made bread, butter, perhaps some pie or sourdough biscuits—all washed down with very hot, very chewy coffee.

And from whence does this grand feast originate? Certainly not from a modern stainless steel galley with microwave and freezer and white-garbed chef, but from a small wood-fired cast-iron stove nestled forward of the mast and tended by the cook—probably the most important man on board. Without a first-rate cook no decent fisherman would put up with the long, hard hours, chancy weather, and sometimes meager shares in the codfishing trade.

Breakfast over, the cook would stand the anchor watch or keep the schooner jogging along over the day's fishing ground as the rest of the crew, including the captain, set out to haul their gear. When they returned in the afternoon, and after the fish were split, gibbed, and salted down, there would be another meal of equal if not greater proportions and variety, sending the men off to a deep if short sleep before starting all over the next day.

Though mostly a fair-weather sailor, I've done some voyaging out in those waters worked by the Banks schooners, and thus harbor no latent romantic desire to slip back in time and sign on merely to avail myself of such a grand moveable feast. But though we may not put in the labor required to consume such Brobdingnagian fare, eating well on the water has to rank high on the rewards of boating. While you could hardly pack a cast-iron Shipmate stove into a beachcruiser, you really can enjoy some grand meals with a minimum of fuss thanks to the high-tech gear and foodstuffs developed for backpackers. You also have a wide array of choices, from gourmet to simple, freeze-dried, or fresh. You also can try your hand at living off the sea—by fishing and foraging.

Nutrition, and More

While today's nutritional experts might take exception with the calorie, cholesterol, or sugar content of the schoonerman's repast, it is still pertinent to understand its value. Food, especially at sea, has three functions: To sustain energy, provide body heat, and lend a psychological boost. Naturally, given the hard physical work of commercial fishing, a diet high in carbohydrates and calories is necessary to sustain energy. Likewise, such a diet provides the fuel for the internal furnace so easily depleted by extended exposure to adverse weather. And before or after the labors of a lonely, sometimes boring, often hazardous occupation, a grand meal provides a strong psychological boost.

In a slightly different fashion, the same rules apply to the recreational boater. While we go boating for fun, we still need sufficient fuel to provide the energy required to perform efficiently and safely on the water. Conditions can conspire to test your strength and skills, and a half-empty stomach becomes a decided liability at such times. Even though most of us will never be out in gale-driven snow, four or five hours of exposure to a steady wind, even on a fine July day that is sweltering ashore, can chill you to the bone; your internal furnace will need fuel. These are both serious needs, and I'll detail their basic requirements shortly, but lest we wax too grim, don't forget the other need: I'll go on record as saying that about half the reason I go sailing is the pleasure of enjoying a fine meal in some fair anchorage after a stimulating, albeit modest, day's voyage.

I'll admit to having subsisted in earlier days on hot dogs, potato chips, soda, Dinty Moore's, and beans—eaten hot or cold depending on circumstance. I believe I have managed to survive to the ripe age of 50 without having eaten a single Twinkie or Devil Dog, but it took some time to develop a sophisticated sailing palate. Happily, today my meals afloat and ashore are better fare for body and soul. While my menu varies depending on where, for how long, and when I am going, trust me that I do not exaggerate when I record in my log book:

> *Sunday August 3rd. Wind SW 10 knots. Left Port Clyde after lunch, saw several seals and a porpoise, made for Graffam Island in Muscle Ridge—12-mile run, nice easy sail accompanied by some Brahms, Brubeck, and Bolling. Anchored late afternoon, seas calm, sunset never fails to inspire. Rowed ashore for some good blue mussels, dropped a bottle of Blanc du Blanc over the side, tied with a string. While the mussels steamed in wine, opened a can of small whole potatoes, sliced and sauteed them with some butter, garlic, and thyme. Topped off with a few slices of tomato and a freeze-dried apple cobbler. Accompanied a cup of rose hip and spearmint tea with a slightly fuzzy reception of the Detroit Symphony. Intended to read, but fell nicely asleep to the gentle rocking of the boat.*

Now if that doesn't invite you to go beachcruising, well, there's always Burger King.

I've described, of course, ideal conditions, yet even if the day has been foul and the anchorage bouncy, with patience and good humor plus a little planning for the event, you can still get together a decent meal. For that matter, even though it may be more difficult to assemble, a good meal is *particularly* imperative after a bad day.

The source of your nutrition is your choice—depending on whether you are a health-food devotee, vegetarian, or a meat-and-potatoes type—but the basic requirements are the same. I'm not saying that the old hot dog, chips, and soda diet will get you drubbed out of the cruising club, but it probably won't sustain you when cruising.

Since you are likely to expend more energy boating than sitting home

watching football, you will need a higher intake of calories and carbohydrates than usual, and probably more protein. Take the time to consider the content of your expected diet, and try to include enough of the essentials. High-sugar foods may give quick energy, but they are empty calories with no staying power. Pasta and grains provide good sustainable carbohydrates. Protein for muscle maintenance can come from a variety of sources, vegetable or meat. Fish might not be as filling, but it seems no accident that its source is close at hand. Focusing on good basic nutrition can lay the base for more gourmet finishes, and while I sometimes still indulge in a bag of chips, it's purely habit—nuts, fruit, popcorn, or even Triscuits are a better snack choice.

By maintaining your body's basic nutritional needs you will have a sense of well-being that will enable you to enjoy your experiences as well as give you the energy reserves to cope with more stressful circumstances that easily can arise on the water. That may sound simplistic, but it is true. Beachcruising by its very nature should be a leisurely, easy-paced activity. Yet if you start out on a weekend cruise after a rotten week at the office, overtired and careless about the food supplies, and by Sunday the weather turns foul, without ample physical reserves an otherwise unpleasant circumstance could become dangerous.

I continue to emphasize safety because being on the water demands it, no matter why you're out there. And while on the subject, I'll fire my last warning salvo: Yo Ho Ho and a Bottle of Rum. While underway it's just plain dumb!

We are fortunate these days to see some small erosion of the macho myth of the two-fisted drinker. Everyone knows that behind the wheel of a car, Joe Six-Pack is a menace. Yet it's equally true behind the helm of a boat. The "operating under the influence" laws of many states now cover marine areas as well, but that alone should not restrain you from overindulgence underway. There's a much better one: That glowing, invincible feeling while surveying the vast blue water, drink in hand, will evaporate in a hurry in an emergency, resulting in poor judgment, slow reflexes, and the possibility of a fatal mistake. Leave the jug corked until the anchor is down. Besides, if beachcruising doesn't give you a natural high anyway, it's unlikely that alcohol will change your perceptions. Maybe you need another form of recreation.

The Ingredients

The ingredients for cruising fare come from three groups: ready-made (cooked ahead and frozen, canned goods, fresh produce, meats and fish), freeze-dried or prepackaged (light, complete backpacker meals, pasta, and other items that need only the addition of water), and foraged (fresh-caught fish, shellfish, wild fruits and vegetables).

If you are new to this activity and are planning more than a one-day trip, deciding on a menu is the most efficient way to develop a realistic provisions list. That might sound obvious, but nothing is worse than being down to soggy saltines, a can of sauerkraut, and a half stick of margarine on the last day out. If you make a menu rather than a separate list for each meal, you will see where things can overlap. Then add enough extras to prepare one of two additional impromptu meals in case weather or whimsy extends your stay. I generally come home with part of what I took along, but being out on the water tends to make most people hungrier than on land.

Obviously you can't take your refrigerator and pantry with you, but you can focus on what will travel well and prepare easily underway. Anything in the fresh or frozen category will need some means of remaining that way, and while there are many ice-chests on the market, how large a one you can handle will be determined by your ability to lug it and stow it aboard your boat without tripping over it.

Decide what is essential to stow on ice—like fresh fish, meat, or dairy products. Some items usually kept in the refrigerator at home need only be stowed in a plastic container away from the sun to keep well for the duration of a casual cruise. These include eggs, margarine, and most "hard" vegetables and fruits such as carrots, beans, potatoes, apples, pears, etc. And unless you are sailing where the water is tepid, drinks can be cooled at anchor by securing them in a net bag and lowering them over the side. Another good trick for other than carbonated beverages is to freeze them in their plastic or paper containers. Kept under cover they will stay cold for at least a day. And a plastic half-gallon jug of frozen juice will cool an ice chest just as effectively as a jug of water.

In keeping with "the in-laws-just-called-and-can't-make-it-this-weekend-what-say-we-just. . . ." style of cruising, rather than waste a precious hour or more shopping or planning, you might keep two or three favorite one-pot entrees prepared ahead and frozen. My wife and I recently took an impromptu three-day canoe trip down the Connecticut River and enjoyed cool gazpacho for lunch, and chicken curry, gourmet chili, and Boeuf Bourguignonne for our dinners, all ready to go, right from our freezer. One cooler, one pot, and no mixing, chopping, or dropping peppers in the sand. Plenty of time for beach strolling or . . . whatever.

And just in case the afternoon sail invites us to stay overnight, I keep a crate of dry goods on board *White Heron*. Nothing fancy, just canned goods, packaged pasta and rice side dishes, and one or two freeze-dried entrees. The secret to making this pedestrian cache palatable is the odd little extras packed in with the beans, sardines, and tuna: A compact spice dispenser with six or seven seasonings—thyme, curry, basil, garlic, oregano, lemon pepper, etc.; and a modest investment from the gourmet section of your local supermarket or fancy goods store—small jars of pimento, black olives, pickles, onions, whatever you like. Now is the time to try some of those odd-looking but tempting goodies you normally pass by.

Even the nondescript package of onion soup mix can add dimension to plain rice or a can of green beans. It isn't even necessary to be too fussy about planning the combinations; invention leads to discovery. Now and then a combination will be better thrown over the side than eaten, but for the most part this "ready box" can give you both freedom and some interesting meals from plain goods.

More and more food items packaged today can be kept without refrigeration. If you are concerned about chemicals and additives, it would be wise to do some careful label reading. Most health-food stores offer sound alternatives, though at usually higher cost, and the packaged supermarket fare has become, under pressure, increasingly healthier and less tainted by polysyllabic preservatives.

Even though the sailor doesn't have to carry his kitchen on his back, the lightweight freeze-dried foods developed for the hiker are a welcome addition to the cruising galley. Perusing the freeze-dried food section of a good outdoors outfitter like REI or L.L. Bean is not unlike window shopping menus in Soho: shrimp scampi, fettucine Alfredo, beef and mushrooms with wild rice, Mandarin orange chicken, lasagna, pasta primavera, Mexican chili, and chicken curry, to name a few. Most require only water; some can even be prepared in the foil pouch they come in. Since they have been developed for a health-conscious group, most are relatively free of unnecessary additives. The cost of an entree currently runs about $5, but this will generally feed two if supplemented with some bread and vegetable or salad. Several desserts such as puddings and cobblers, are offered too.

And what about the water you'll need for those freeze-dried delicacies? Sadly, more often than not, the water isn't safe to drink, even in the wilderness. Some remote lakes or rivers may be free of contaminates, but being miles from the nearest doctor is no time to find out. Hauling potable water may be inconvenient, but it's the absolute best bet. Barring that, boiling the devil out of it, so to speak, along with purifying it with Halazone tablets or the like is your next best defense. There is a water purifier on the market known as "First Need" that uses a replaceable filter to remove, its manufacturer says, disease-bearing bacteria, Giardia, parasites, toxic chemicals, and pesticides—without chemicals or boiling. It can purify one quart of water in 90 seconds. The unit is bulky and costs about $30, but it is considered reliable in moderately polluted waters.

If you are near municipalities, I'd opt for carrying your own water—industrial and commercial waste is serious stuff and hard to filter out. This may seem depressing if you've imagined sailing or motoring up some inviting river or bay and drinking the cool, clear waters that always seem for some reason to be featured in beer commercials. Lugging your own water may have a hidden virtue, too—it makes you more aware of the impact our modern civilization has had on the environment, and in just a couple of hundred short years.

Most of us like to start the day with a hot beverage, and there are those for whom a day just will not get moving without a decent cup of coffee. A lukewarm mug of instant just won't do. I've found that a small supply of fresh-ground, a simple funnel and paper filter, and a good thermos solves the problem. The thermos—the type with a pump top is ideal—keeps you from having to light another fire for the inevitable second cup.

While on the subject of breakfast, remember that it is your basic fuel supply for the day and should be substantial. It can be grain, fruit, and nut, or more traditional. If you are not carrying fresh milk, orange juice works just as well with cold cereal. Powdered milk (most backpackers seem to favor Milkman brand) works fine with quick-cooking oatmeal.

Since you seldom have a whole stove-top and several pots to cook with, I've found that I can saute basic ingredients such as corned beef, onions, canned potatoes, then pour beaten eggs over the top, perhaps with some grated cheese and spices. Since most camp-stoves are not hay-burners, you can cover the pan and simmer gently until the eggs are set, or scramble the ingredients. It might not be picture perfect, but it makes a hearty one-pot breakfast.

If you plan to be underway at lunchtime, it makes sense to do most of the preparations ahead of time. Soup will keep well in a thermos, and you can drink it from a mug. A good soup makes a good lunch—and provides another area to be creative. Start with some basic mix, broth, or canned soup, and fortify it with other canned goods such as beans, peas, carrots, pasta, or rice. I tend to like my soup on the chewy side—more akin to stew, which is also easier to eat on a pitching boat. Add some crusty rolls and a banana or some dried fruit and nuts for a balanced meal.

Sandwiches are justifiably popular at lunch, but no matter what the filling, nothing, I mean absolutely nothing, is less appetizing than a soggy sandwich. Unless the filling is extra moist, Syrian bread pockets are ideal; they can be eaten with one hand and don't spill into the bilge. Otherwise, make up the fixings and add the bread later. That way, if it turns out too bouncy to make the sandwiches, you can just eat the tuna salad or whatever right out of the bowl.

Fishing and Foraging

It is curious, and possibly alarming, that in America roughly three percent of the population produce the food for the other 97 percent. We are so used to obtaining most of our food from the market that the notion of getting anything from the original source seems abstract at best. If you live in an urban area, it's almost impossible even to try, but even in less artificial surroundings our busy lives leave few of us with the time to raise crops or livestock or hunt for wild plants to supplement our diets. For the few days or even weeks of beachcruising, living in a more natural environment, it may not change our lives to learn to live off the land and sea but I think it will help temper our awareness as well as provide some interesting and refreshing new dining experiences. The labor involved in procuring such meals will be rewarded by both a sense of involvement and self-reliance. However, until you gain some level of experience at it, I don't think I'd recommend setting off without backup supplies. Even the early wilderness traveler usually had along some flour, salt, and bacon to fall back on if the hunting or fishing was thin.

Cruising might afford those who have done little or no fishing the opportunity to try it. A fresh-caught anything, pan fried with some potatoes or whatever, might just make an avid angler out of a former fish-hater. Obviously this can't be a comprehensive treatise on fishing, but it may get you started.

Inquire locally or, if time permits, to the state conservation department, as to what fish are common and what licenses and laws apply, and select your gear accordingly. The barest minimum for the minimally interested are the collapsible fishing outfits available from discount stores and late-night TV ads. A fish of any size, however, will make short work of them. For small boats with room for nothing else, better-quality collapsible outfits are available from sporting goods stores.

If you have more room, the most foolproof rig for all-around use is a closed-face spin-casting outfit ($35 or so), about $5^1/2$ feet long, equipped with 10-pound test line. That should handle most anything you're likely to encounter in the casual kind of fishing we're talking about.

If you happen to be in deep saltwater, don't bother with an oversized boat rod, use what the old timers did: a hand line. Cod line wound on a simple wooden reel (available in any coastal sporting goods or hardware store) twisted hand over hand will lower a heavy sinker and a hook baited with a mussel or clam down to the depths where the big ones swim, and

123

with a little patience and perseverance, will drag them back up. This same rig works fine for the catfish that inhabit the freshwater of the South and Midwest. A local derivation, "juggin," mounts the baited line on a jug that is set adrift (check local laws first), with the bait dangling near the bottom. When the jug starts moving against the current or bobs under, you've got supper.

But the easiest, most carefree way to catch fish, whether in fresh or salt water, is trolling, either with a hand-line or a rod in a holder (about $10) clamped to the boat. Since you're just jogging along anyway, there's little to it: just stream the appropriate lure astern (always use a swivel between the lure and line to prevent twisting), carry on with your business, and keep an eye on the line for action. Most species can be taken this way: In salt water, mackerel (delicious grilled) and harbor pollack are common, along with the occasional bluefish (if bluefish are known to be in your area, you'll need stouter equipment—at least 20-pound–test line and wire leaders to fend off their razor-sharp teeth). In fresh water, depending on location, trout, salmon, bass, and walleyed pike can be taken while trolling. Local sporting goods stores can point you toward the right lures, but the Swedish Rapalas in a variety of sizes and colors seem to work everywhere for everything, as do the ubiquitous red-and-white spoons.

SHELLFISHING

There was a time, dear reader, when lobsters were so plentiful that if you wanted a dozen or so for supper, you sent a boy down to the shore with a gaff hook to root them out from around the inshore ledges; it certainly wasn't grownup's work. And lobster was no delicacy, either, but common fare for common people. Times change. If you are sailing the New England coast nowadays, I'm afraid you'll have to buy your lobsters. Don't even think of poaching from a trap—lobstermen have their own version of justice out on the water—though sometimes you can buy one or two direct from a fisherman out hauling if you are polite and haven't just run over his pot warps.

Lobsters excepted, most other shellfish can be foraged, and at least in small quantities for personal consumption, without license (check your local ordinances). In salt water areas you can find several varieties of clams, oysters, crabs, mussels, scallops, shrimp, and if you have a taste for the exotic, sea urchins.

One precaution: On occasion, the taking of shellfish from a particu-

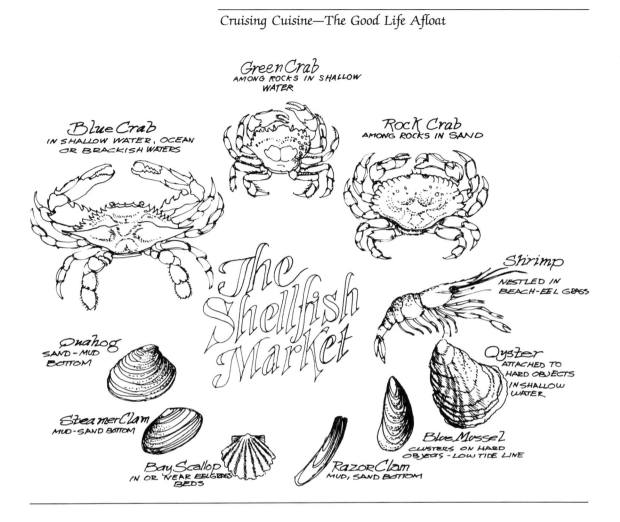

Green Crab
AMONG ROCKS IN SHALLOW
WATER

Blue Crab
IN SHALLOW WATER, OCEAN
OR BRACKISH WATERS

Rock Crab
AMONG ROCKS IN SAND

The Shellfish Market

Shrimp
NESTLED IN
BEACH-EEL GRASS

Quahog
SAND - MUD
BOTTOM

Oyster
ATTACHED TO
HARD OBJECTS
IN SHALLOW
WATER

Steamer Clam
MUD - SAND BOTTOM

Blue Mussel
CLUSTERS ON HARD
OBJECTS - LOW TIDE LINE

Bay Scallop
IN OR NEAR EELGRASS
BEDS

Razor Clam
MUD, SAND BOTTOM

lar area is banned for a specific interval. It may result from pollution, a naturally occurring red tide—which renders the shellfish poisonous, or because the area may have suffered overfishing. You should be aware of the potential for this and find out if it may apply in your area at any given time. NOAA weather radio usually mentions areas closed by red tide or pollution; most other closed areas have warning signs on the bank (although you may not see them if you approach from the sea).

Oysters, quahogs and scallops may be eaten raw, and save for the sea

125

urchins, the rest should be cooked. Though plentiful in New England coastal waters, this spiny shellfish has been ignored by Americans. However, it has long been a delicacy, known as *uni*, in Japan. It is now being harvested here and shipped whole to the orient, where the roe is extracted and eaten raw like caviar. A friend of mine described the taste as something like salty oatmeal. To each his own.

Please, even if you find a great abundance of species in an area, do not collect more than you can eat; they may seem to be just lying about, but once you have picked them up they cannot survive, even if dumped back in the water later on. If you have trouble judging what you need, blue mussels, for example, usually found in great quantities, make a suitable meal at roughly a pound in the shell per person.

So much for the main course, but while you are wandering about the shoreline you just might want to pick up a salad, some vegetables, and maybe dessert. They don't come brightly labeled, but then there's no check-out at this supermarket either. There are more edible plants, nuts, and berries in almost any location than you imagine. It would take a whole volume to describe them here, but I'll show you some of the more common types; if you become hooked there are good books on the subject, many specific to your area.

FORAGING

With the exception of the few wild edibles we are familiar with in domestic form, some of the foraged plants will taste unusual at first; some you may acquire a taste for and others you'll discard, but I've found a few that are well worth the hunting. The only hard and fast rule is that if you cannot positively identify a plant, don't eat it. Very few are really poisonous, but there are some serious exceptions and you are a long way from medical help.

Milkweed and Dandelion Greens. Here are two plants that are found almost everywhere, and yet few people would think of eating them. Collect the wooly clusters of the milkweed flower buds while they are still green; boiled or steamed they taste like broccoli. Very young dandelion leaves make good salad greens—usually in May and June. Older greens can be cooked as a pot herb for a nutritious tea.

Beach Peas. Found along cobble beaches, these vegetables have oval leaves that come to a sharp point on the tip. The plant has thick stems that curl

Blackberry

Blueberry

Rosehip

The Green-Grocer

Red Raspberry

Dandelion

Milkweed

Beach Pea

and spread over the ground for several feet. The youngest leaves make a good salad ingredient and the small pods are like snow peas and can be eaten whole. When the pods turn yellow the peas must be removed (a time-consuming project since they are quite small), but dried beach peas have a nut-like taste and may be made into a soup.

Wild Rose. This seaside rose grows in dense clumps up to eight feet tall. In early summer their main value is to fragrantly grace your cruising table, but from August through October the fruit, which looks a little like a cherry tomato, appears. This small red fruit has the highest concentration of Vitamin C in the world. You can make a stimulating and health-giving tea of them by cutting the slightly softened rose hips in half; scrape out the seeds and hair and dry the pieces in the sun. Steep the dried hips in hot but not boiling water (boiling diminishes the potency of the vitamin content). They can be eaten raw as well, though they are quite tart — a few mixed with other berries make a good dessert.

Strawberries, Raspberries, Blackberries, and Blueberries. We are all familiar with these delicacies, found in a wide range of island and coastal areas, usually in late July and August. While you are gathering them, take your foraging field guide along. You may find other, less-familiar species of edible plants and herbs.

Foraging is not just limited to the high-tide line: some of the seaweed is also edible, and although an acquired taste, it has high levels of vitamins and protein. Dried dulse is sold commercially. In Eastern Canada it is popular as a sort of natural potato chip — with a strong aftertaste, but quite palatable once you are used to it. Dulse, recognized by its purplish hand-shaped fronds, generally about eight inches long, is collected at dead low water.

In the kelp family, alaria, dried and added to other herbs as a high-iodine and vitamin seasoning, recently has become a commercial product as well. Also harvested at very low tides, alaria has long, wavy "leaves" up to three feet long. Although some can grow up to three yards in New England, the West Coast variety can reach 100 feet. Kelp fronds should be cut free, not pulled, as new growth will regenerate if the root system is left intact. The midrib section of alaria can be sliced like a carrot and added to salads, or boiled like a vegetable.

This is just a slight taste of the wild, and it may not be your cup of tea, herbal or otherwise, but it has been my experience that a meal foraged all or in part from the shoreline provides not only a new taste experience but contributes to a better appreciation of the natural world around us. We may have moved far afield from the day when we can individually live off the land, but some experiences in self sufficiency can add perspective in a world where the food chain becomes ever more synthesized every day.

CHAPTER Six

Two Cruises

Freedom is a hard thing to define. This book is dedicated to the ideas that less is more and the best experiences are freestyle, yet its chapters are filled with procedures, cautions, and pragmatisms. One doesn't seem to exist without the other—the ways and means of our activities shape them no matter how simple we try to keep them. I have tried to illustrate some of the practical considerations that give the beachcruiser a base from which to exercise his or her own options. Thus rather than trying to end the book with the ultimate definition, I would like just to share a little of my own experiences on the water.

An Island Storm

For most of my sailing life I have cruised solo—not that I have any great propensity for being alone, but until I met my wife I had not found a compatible companion. Compatibility needn't mean similarity. She is earth rooted and I am waterborne. By cruising among the islands and bays of Maine we complement each other and share new experiences. Yet there is always a time for aloneness — by choice. Since my sharpie is really too small for two anyway, it makes the ideal solo boat. It is small enough for me to drag ashore, and seaworthy enough to make island hopping reasonably safe.

Generally, late September on the coast is a fine time on the water — the fog is largely gone, as are most of the tourists, the winds become steadier as the land mass cools, yet I'm always amazed at the number of boats religiously hauled out right after Labor Day. Though there can be surprises, Indian Summer mostly provides clear sunny days, moderate breezes, and spectacular foliage.

On such a fine, promising weekend I sailed downriver, my sharpie loaded with a couple of new meals I wanted to try and a half-finished manuscript I thought could benefit from some fresh air and space. The tide and a quiet northwesterly pushed me out past Port Clyde, and I decided to make for Otter Island a few miles off to the southwest. NOAA reported 10-15 knots NW with possible higher gusts, and the sky was nearly cloudless.

I thought I'd stop for lunch at Otter and then maybe work across Muscongus Bay to check out a new overnight spot I'd been told about on Thief Island. By 11 I was abreast the small cove on the southern end of Otter, and I noticed that the wind was kicking up whitecaps behind me. Because a ledge makes out on the eastern approach, I had to sail a little past to get into the cove, which meant an upwind tack, and when I came about I realized that the wind was much stronger than I had expected. This is often the case when you are running downwind; you don't really feel the force of it until you round up.

Sharpies don't point high, and it took some heads-up sailing to make the short distance into the cove, but once inside the water was quieter, and I could easily beach the boat. I hauled out my galley box and heated some thick minestrone my wife had kindly provided me with — a gentle but pleasant reminder of her presence on my short solo odyssey.

Nestled below the fir trees on the rocky beach, I could relax in the warm sunshine, but I could see the tops of the branches swaying, and I had a feeling I would not be going anywhere after lunch. I pulled the boat higher up on the shelf above high tide line and secured it with the anchor line to a sturdy tree, and decided to take a walk along the island's perimeter.

The island's nearly impenetrable vegetation made walking through it nearly impossible, and I had to scramble around the broken granite edges to make the half-mile to the island's northern end. By the time I got there the wind had picked up to at least 25 or 30 knots, and fast-moving gray cirrus clouds moved in overhead. Now and then a gust would nearly knock me from my feet, and I decided to sit down on a small outcropping, my back against a spruce tree.

As I watched the approaching storm, my first thoughts were of my wife, who would be looking out at the same weather and wondering. We had talked about such things of course, and I could take some comfort in the knowledge that she had faith in my judgment and would know I'd more than likely hole up somewhere safe. Still, it's times like this that make one wish, however briefly, for a cellular telephone or even a CB radio. After a while, though, I began to focus on the storm itself. Some small birds flew inland for protection just as a lobsterboat motored past on its way home. These fishermen work regularly in all kinds of weather, of course, and I tried to assure myself that they had just finished hauling traps for the day and were headed home, and were not urgently seeking shelter. Yet as I watched them go out of sight, throwing spray as they crested each wave, I felt very lonely indeed.

Then, for some reason, Debussy's *La Mer* came into my head. I have this odd ability to "play" extended works in my mind, and as the wind began to sting my cheeks, forcing me to turtle down into my foul weather gear, I became mesmerized by the blending of the sights and sounds before me accompanied by the lush, emotional orchestral colorings in my mind. As I witnessed the strange beauty of the storm I thought of man's ability to reflect it in art. The rocks below became obscured in the spray; more than once a fine mist covered me, though I was well above them.

The day had been warm, but I soon began to shiver, and wished I had some hot coffee or tea with me. For the moment I could not move, however. Walking back along the rocks would be too risky, and ploughing through the undergrowth too much work. My mind blew abstract images past—what it would be like out there in my little sharpie, how secure we are most of the time in our "habitats," how small and vulnerable man really is. Not necessarily revolutionary, profound, or original thinking, but the experience was direct, not on film or in a book. Despite lingering anxieties that I could not communicate with my wife, I found a certain cleansing in the storm, and gratitude for having experienced it.

It was hardly the storm of the century; by evening it had moderated, though it continued to blow a good 20 knots until around midnight. I made my way back to the sharpie and watched the sun go down as I fixed supper: freeze-dried lasagna—not good, though not bad. At least it was warm, and I was very tired. With the boom tent up I fell into a deep sleep, manuscript forgotten, with the trees providing background music. Nature

133

called about one, and I climbed out into a very still, incredibly starlit night.

At this time of year it can, of course, blow for days, and I might have had to face a repeat the next morning. But even if NOAA had underestimated yesterday's wind, on the whole their satellite data can predict overall patterns and air mass movements with reasonable accuracy. Had they forecast an extended low-pressure system, for instance, I would never have gone in the first place. As it turned out, the storm had taken most of the wind with it, the morning was still flat calm, and I lingered over a leisurely breakfast of a Swiss cheese omelet, fried potatoes, and spearmint and rose-hip tea. I looked over that bit of writing I'd brought along, and if the storm had not exactly given me blinding insight into the mysteries of the universe, it at least had left me with a bit clearer vision of what I was trying to write—even though it had nothing to do with the sea.

By 10 a nice southeasterly arose, and as I sailed by the north end of the island I couldn't help contrast the quiet, undisturbed appearance of my storm perch today with its very different appearance only a few hours before. Such is the rhythm of nature: It goes on in its cyclical fashion, undisturbed, yet sometimes our lives are forever altered by it. I thought of all the sailors and fishermen lost in storms, and how the sea remains an awesome power as well as a remarkable and beautiful environment.

Though weather and circumstances are always different, I enjoy my one or two solos each year. I would imagine each of us takes such journeys for different reasons but the return always leaves me refreshed, better able to keep perspective on whatever worldly concerns I may have. Getting away from it all is a good reason for a brief solo—*running* away from it all is not.

It was good to see Irma walking down to the shore with our dog, and good to know her anxieties had been fleeting and her own time alone had been spent peacefully working in her garden.

An Island in Time

We had a rare week to ourselves and the weather seemed promising, so we spread out the charts and mapped an itinerary. Normally, since our cruising is just for a day or two, we head out and let the wind take us to any number of what have become familiar and favorite spots in either Muscongus Bay or Muscle Ridge. Since we had more time it might be worth sailing "uphill" for a day to Damariscove Island, a few miles south of Boothbay Harbor. From there we could explore several anchorages for a few days and then hopefully ride the southwesterly home.

We were looking at a 30-mile trip, so we motored *White Heron* out at dawn to get south of Port Clyde before the morning breeze began. With its winged keel and efficient rig, the *Heron* made the day of long tacks an easy one, and by four in the afternoon we had Damariscove off the starboard beam and could easily make the island on a reach.

Now and then you get grand days when the sea conditions are perfectly matched to your boat. This was such a day. Several porpoises kept us company for a while, and Irma had a grand snooze in the capacious cockpit—I was even able to tack without disturbing her.

Damariscove Island is really two islands joined in the middle by a narrow rock ledge—the whole being two miles long by a half-mile wide. The southern end contains a narrow harbor where the now-deserted

135

DAMARISCOVE STATION

Coast Guard station sits on the southwestern point. The northern end is covered by brush and forms a protected nesting area for eider ducks. The island is currently under the management of the Nature Conservancy, which maintains a summer monitoring program.

The island once was home to a community of 40 or 50 people, and had been inhabited until around 1930 for more than 300 years. It was this fact that brought us there, and subsequently the reason we abandoned our earlier plans to explore other islands in the region. But then, that is the beauty of cruising—we had no social obligations, and unlike a tour of Europe with eleven countries "seen" in nine days, just because we got there by boat did not mean we had to be underway at first light to another destination.

We had a small book written by a former island resident outlining the island's history and containing some wonderful glimpses into island life. For current interest, there was all the flora and fauna of the now all-but-deserted community. Thus this cruise might be a little different from some, but it would be a wonderful time-out for the two of us—time to talk quietly together, certainly time for a little romance and a leisurely exploration of the shore and heath, and time to imagine past lives and times.

First settled in 1622 when British fishermen established a drying station for salt cod, Damariscove went through a long succession of ownership and uses. There were Indian battles (the source, some say, of a headless ghost), farming and homesteading, and later a resort community flourished here. In 1897 a life-saving station was erected—a grand building that still stands, though after the Coast Guard left in 1959 it was vandalized and only recently restored. I spent two days making drawings of it and imagining the life it contained, and later wrote a fictional account of one of the local men who had worked in the service, based on my impressions and on diaries and logs from Damariscove's Life-Saving Station. It is included here not so much because it has anything to do with cruising, but because I think the opportunity to know such things and visit where they took place is one of the nobler aspects of this avocation. Somehow it makes me feel connected, a part of the life that repeats and repeats at the water's edge.

We had a lot of drills, setting up the breeches buoy, running out the surfboats, and practicing rowing in the choppy water around ledges and rocks. Capt. Godfrey, our leader, worked us hard. We had a lot of time to ourselves though. I liked to go up and talk to one of the Poole boys running the sheep farm, as it was kind of like home, except there was almost no trees. The islanders that live here all the time were friendly to most of us, but I don't know how they stood it, being here all their lives. I got kind of fond of one of the girls who lived over to the White House at the head of the harbor, but her old man kept her close to home.

I had to stand watch in the Tower, the lookout on the high ground on the other side of the harbor. You could see most everywhere from there, even to Monhegan, and at night you could catch most of the lights on this part of the coast.

In the winter it didn't snow much but it was awful cold. We still had to drill though, and of course with the weather so foul there was always some boat or other in trouble so we had to work. But we had a nice place to live. Somebody told me it was the grandest station around, even though our bunk room got cold right through. But from the outside, the place looked like one of the summer houses down to Boothbay.

The other day we were just finishing breakfast. Capt. Godfrey was sitting with us and we had our usual good stuff—eggs, bread, biscuits, ham, a couple of pork chops, strong coffee, and some fresh-made codfish cakes. Sometimes, like on a specially cold morning as it was this day, there'd be some pie or gingerbread too.

It was blowing for dear outside and there was sea smoke in it, a

137

raw damp day such as we had had for two weeks. Billy was over to the Tower on watch, and he came running in all out of breath and said he'd spotted a sloop up on Fisherman's Ledge, and though he couldn't see her very well he knew she was taking a pounding and her crew couldn't last if they was to go in the water.

We all scrambled downstairs to the boatshed. It's quite a sight, that shed, made of granite stones and able to stand up to any beating by big waves that are always crashing up beside it on account of it was built right on the ledge next to the harbor mouth. Our lifeboat was on a kind of railway car so we could get right down to the water quick. We could row that thing, but we also had a new engine—a 5-h.p. Victor, and the Captain got her going almost before we hit the water. I don't know much about boats, and to tell the truth when I first saw this lifeboat I couldn't figure how we could ever be safe in big waves, but I'll tell you, whoever figured her out knew what he was doing.

First of all, she had scuppers, they called 'em, which let the water that came aboard go right out again, mostly. The first time I was in her, we pushed out with the wind coming at us from the east like she was today, and I figured we'd bury the bow, but I quick got to trust her because she just rose up and acted like she was some kind of fish riding the waves.

The Captain pushed the tiller over hard and we swung back to northwest, in towards the ledges, and we were surfing with the wind at our backs, making seven or eight knots easy. I lost one of my mittens getting aboard and my hand was near froze, but I tried to think of the crew of that sloop out there on the ledge.

It only took us about 20 minutes to get there. We could see the stern—she was pitching up and down, and it looked like her bow was stove in. Her crew was in the stern hanging on to the rail. There were three I could see, but it looked like there might be another on the deck by the way one of the others was bending over. Captain was some skilled when it came to handling a boat, and being shoal draft we could work ourselves around those ledges, especially since he knew these waters. He brought us up to the lee of her—we had two oars out, sort of sculling sideways to try to hold her to. The sea was really up and it was hard going. Me and Billy heaved a line over to her but one of her crew, a young man, was waving his arms and yelling, and he jumped right in the water. I guess he was afraid because the boat was pitching badly and on the point of breaking up.

I grabbed his jacket, but my hand was so cold I couldn't hold on. Billy caught him just as he started to float past, and we hauled him over the rail. He'd of drowned in another minute. I could see now that one of the others was a woman—they seemed to be a family. I wondered what they was doing out in weather like this—mostly only fishermen would do that. We got the woman and what I guessed must be her father over pretty easy as they did what we told 'em. Then the Captain ordered us to get close alongside, and he grabbed the rail and heaved himself on board to tend to the man lying on the rear deck. There was some blood on the fellow's face, but it was so cold the bleeding had stopped. It was hard to get him overside and into our pitching lifeboat, but we all had worked at learning how to do this and we pulled away just as the sloop took another lurch and more water poured through her stove-in planking. We put the injured down in the bilge—guess he was the woman's husband the way she was carrying on—and headed back. We took some pounding going back as now the wind was dead on us. It took nearly an hour, but we came around the point pretty good and Billy and I jumped on the ramp so we could hook up the cables to pull the boat back into the shed.

We got everybody inside and warmed up. The cook had more strong coffee and a little rum to go with it, and he'd fixed up some biscuits and ham while we was gone. Seemed the crew of the sloop was a family named Miller from Small Point Harbor and they'd been headed down to Port Clyde because of a death in the family. The injured man, Walter, had been sailing while the family was below—the boom jibed and hit him down and the others couldn't handle the helm so they wound up on the ledge. We put them up at the White House till the weather was good enough for a boat to come for them. Guess their sloop pounded to bits, we didn't see it again.

"The Journal of Willy Payson" first appeared in *Island Journal*.

While I dreamed of bygone days, my wife carefully scoured the island for several good and interesting meals. We had an assortment of wild salads, and good blue mussels (they seemed to be everywhere), but the piece de resistance was periwinkle chowder. Let me tell you that it takes remarkable patience and devotion to make a chowder out of periwinkles. First you have to boil or steam them, then pick a minuscule bit of meat out of its tiny shell, then add a few potatoes, milk, thyme, and wild celery. I am humbled by Irma's labors for this meal, and if not exactly overstuffed at its conclusion, I felt honored by the offering.

My wife the naturalist is also a great follower of scat, also known by another, more impolite term, but suffice it to say that by following such an interest one finds wildlife that one might otherwise not expect to see. In this case it turned out to be muskrats—hundreds of them living in a series of burrows at the north end of the island. And as we were here after nesting season (and thus allowed to roam freely), we saw dozens of eider families, testifying to the Nature Conservancy's careful husbandry of the island.

By the time we left our snug harbor we'd about used up the week, but it was well worth it. Not to wax too sublime about the experience— we had to pay our dues halfway home as the wind shifted just enough to give us a wet, bouncy ride, and when we finally got into position to take advantage of it for the run up to our cove, the wind all but died on an ebbing tide. Well, that's why we have engines, isn't it?

They say that when you've said all you know, or think you know, stop talking and go home. Thus I shall, leaving you to your own devices. I hope I've invited you to try this less hurried, less expensive, and in my view wonderful way of messing about in boats.

I wish you fair winds and following seas.

BOATS

Sail

West Wight Potter 15' and 19'
HMS Marine
904 W. Hyde Park Boulevard
Inglewood, CA 90302

Com-pac 16' and 19'
Hutchins Company
1195 Kapp Drive
Clearwater, FL 33515

Marsh Hen 17'
Mirage Fiberglass
P.O. Drawer 1989
Palatka, FL 32078

Nordica 16' and 20'
Nordica Yachts Limited
Highway 14
Mount Brydges, Box 339
Ontario, CANADA NOL 1WO

Montgomery 15' and 17'
Montgomery Marine
3236 Fitzgerald Road, Unit 1
Rancho Cordova, CA 95670

Seaward 18'
Starboard Yacht Company
4550 S.E. Hampton Court
Stuart, FL 34997

Sovereign 17'
Custom Fiberglass Products of
Florida Inc.
8136 Leo Kidd Avenue
Port Richey, FL 34668

Dovekie 21'
Edey & Duff
129 Aucoot Road
Mattapoisett, MA 02730

Drascombe Boats 15', 18', and 21'
Honor Marine / Downeast
Drascombe
RR 3 Box 3033
Brunswick, ME 04011

Nimble Boats 20'
Nimble Boats
6135 142nd Avenue North
Clearwater, FL 34620

Capri 16' and 18'
Catalina Sailboats Inc.
21200 Victory Boulevard
Woodland Hills, CA 91367

Sea Pearl 21'
Marine Concepts
159 Oakwood Street East
Tarpon Springs, FL 34689

Beetle Cat 12'
Concordia Company
South Dartmouth, MA 02748

Marshall 17' and 21'
Marshall Marine Corporation
Box P-266
South Dartmouth, MA 02748

Nancy's China Custom Wood 15'
Devlin Designing Boatbuilders
2431 Gravelly Beach Loop N.W.
Olympia, WA 98502

Cornish Shrimper 23'
Britannia Boats
P.O. Box 477
Severna Park, Maryland 21146

Point Jude 16'
Starwing Inc.
P.O. Box 137
Bristol, Rhode Island 02809

Norwalk Island Sharpie 18' (plans
only)
213 Rowayton Avenue
Rowayton, CT 06853

Heron 19' Sharpie
Stephen Wilce Boats
P.O. Box 962
Winters, CA 95694

Power
Boston Whaler 16'6"
Boston Whaler Inc.
1149 Hingham Street
Rockland, MA 02370

Pulsifer Hampton 22'
Richard S. Pulsifer
RFD 3045
Brunswick, ME 04011

Grumman Sportboat 15'
Grumman Boats
Marathon, NY 13803

Pointer 17'
Pointer Boats
Box 721
Yarmouth, ME 04906

Lund 18'
Lund Boats
P.O. Box 248
New York Mills, MN 56567

Multihulls
Tramp Trimaran
Ian Farrier, designer
P.O. Box 7362
Chula Vista, CA 92012

Discovery 20' Trimaran
Chris White Designs
South Dartmouth, MA 02748

Tiki 21 Catamaran
James Wharram Designs
Binary Boat Systems
P.O. Box 22342
Fort Lauderdale, FL 33335

SOME GOOD BOOKS

Sailing America
A Trailer Sailor's Guide to North America
Larry Brown
International Marine Publishing
1990
Camden, Maine

Build the New Instant Boats
Harold "Dynamite" Payson
International Marine Publishing
1984

Open Boat Cruising
Frank and Margaret Dye
David and Charles Press 1982
Pomfret, Vermont

The Practical Pilot
Coastal Navigation by Eye,
Intuition, and Common Sense
Leonard Eyges
International Marine Publishing
1989

Upgrading Your Small Sailboat for Cruising
Paul and Marya Butler
International Marine Publishing
1988

On the Water
The Romance and Lore of America's Small Boats
Douglas Alvord
Yankee Books 1988
Camden, Maine

The Handbook for Beach Strollers: From Maine to Cape Hatteras
Donald Zinn
The Globe Pequot Press 1985
Chester, Connecticut

Cruising Guides
A Cruising Guide to the Maine Coast, Second Edition
Hank and Jan Taft
International Marine Publishing
1991

Cruising the Pacific Coast
Carolyn and Jack West
Pacific Search Press 1984
Seattle, Washington

A Cruising Guide to the Tennessee River, Tenn-Tom Waterway, and the Lower Tombigbee River
Marian, Thomas, and W.J. Rumsey
International Marine Publishing
1991

Cruising the Chesapeake: A Gunkholer's Guide
William Shellenberger
International Marine Publishing
1990

Cruising Guide to Coastal South Carolina, 1985
Clairborne Young
John S. Blair, Publisher
Winston-Salem, North Carolina

Cruising Florida
Red Marston
Ziff-Davis Publishing Company
1981
New York, New York

Outfitters

Although we refer in this book to specific gear for camping, cooking, navigation, and safety, most manufacturers will not sell their products directly. The best alternative is to request a catalog from a firm specializing in outdoor gear. Three of the best are: L.L. Bean of Freeport, Maine, 1-800-341-4341; Cabela's Incorporated of Sidney, Nebraska, 308-254-5505; and Recreational Equipment Incorporated of Seattle, Washington, 1-800-426-4840.

For specific marine products, your local marine supply house or chandlery is a good place to compare products, though there are some good discount mail order houses, such as E & B Discount Marine in Providence, Rhode Island, 1-800-533-5007; or West Marine Products in Watsonville, California, 1-800-538-0775.

Index